Francis Brooks

Greek Lyric Poets

Francis Brooks

Greek Lyric Poets

ISBN/EAN: 9783744781428

Printed in Europe, USA, Canada, Australia, Japan

Cover: Foto ©ninafisch / pixelio.de

More available books at **www.hansebooks.com**

GREEK LYRIC POETS

SELECTED AND TRANSLATED BY

FRANCIS BROOKS, M.A.

LECTURER IN CLASSICS AT UNIVERSITY
COLLEGE, BRISTOL, AND FORMERLY CLASSICAL
SCHOLAR OF BALLIOL COLLEGE, OXFORD

LONDON: DAVID NUTT
270-271 STRAND
1896

Edinburgh: T. and A. CONSTABLE, Printers to Her Majesty

INTRODUCTION

THE text made use of in this selection from the Lyric poets of Greece is that of Bergk in the fourth edition of his *Poetae Lyrici Graeci*. The very few instances in which that text has been departed from, either by the adoption of one of Bergk's own conjectures, or of one of the well-known readings of other scholars, have been indicated in a foot-note. I have also followed Bergk in the order of the fragments. The figures within brackets represent the numbering in his edition.

Except in the case of Archilochus and Tyrtaeus the selections have been made from Bergk's third volume. Archilochus and Tyrtaeus are placed in his second volume, the former amongst the iambic poets, the latter amongst the elegiac. But Archilochus ranks so naturally with lyric writers that I have followed the example of Mr. Farnell in his *Greek Lyric Poetry* in including extracts from the lyric portion of his work, and also in introducing the two remaining lyric fragments of Tyrtaeus. The iambic verse of Archilochus I have, for the sake of uniformity, not taken into account, but it did not seem worth while to also exclude two or three isolated iambic fragments from other poets.

No elegiac passages have been inserted. The greater number of those contained in the third volume of Bergk are either epigrams or epitaphs, and therefore alien to the nature of the lyric, and the elegiac metre is in itself of so marked a type, and has such widely different associations and effects from those of the lyric, that their introduction would have been doubly incongruous. The Anacreontea have also been omitted. They are of quite late date, and, though by no means devoid of merit, their fluent completeness would have tended to outweigh the much higher poetical excellence of the genuine fragments of Anacreon.

In making this selection I have endeavoured to include nothing that did not possess at least some claim to notice. The contents of the book will be found to deal with most of the chief subjects of human interest,—life, death, fate, religion, national glory, war, politics, love and feasting, the sports of the athlete, and the poet's art. Old-world ritual and invocations, and the games and songs of children are also represented. A curious instance of literary jealousy is exhibited in the feud amongst the dithyrambic poets between the advocates respectively of the flute and the lyre.

I should like to express my obligations to Mr. Farnell's commentary and introductions; all must feel how great a loss to classical studies has been involved in his premature death. Mr. Wharton's book on Sappho I read with much pleasure when it first came out, but have purposely consulted very little in connection with the present translation.

F. BROOKS.

CONTENTS

	PAGE		PAGE
Tyrtaeus	2	Lamprocles	137
Archilochus	4	Pratinas	138
Eumelus	15	Phrynichus	141
Terpander	16	Diagoras	142
Alcman	19	Cydias	143
Arion	33	Praxilla	144
Sappho	36	Bacchylides	146
Alcaeus	60	Melanippides	157
Pittacus	75	Ariphron	160
Bias	75	Licymnius	162
Chilo	75	Philoxenus	163
Thales	76	Timotheus	165
Stesichorus	77	Telestes	169
Ibycus	84	Lycophronides	172
Anacreon	91	Castorio	173
Simonides	110	Scolia	174
Timocreon	130	Carmina Popularia	182
Corinna	135	Fragmenta Adespota	193

ALPHABETICAL LIST OF CONTENTS

	PAGE		PAGE
Alcaeus	60	Licymnius	162
Alcman	19	Lycophronides	172
Anacreon	91	Melanippides	157
Archilochus	4	Philoxenus	163
Arion	33	Phrynichus	141
Ariphron	160	Pittacus	75
Bacchylides	146	Pratinas	138
Bias	75	Praxilla	144
Carmina Popularia	182	Sappho	36
Castorio	173	Scolia	174
Chilo	75	Simonides	110
Corinna	135	Stesichorus	77
Cydias	143	Telestes	169
Diagoras	142	Terpander	16
Eumelus	15	Thales	76
Fragmenta Adespota	193	Timocreon	130
Ibycus	84	Timotheus	165
Lamprocles	137	Tyrtaeus	2

GREEK LYRIC POETS

I

A

TYRTAEUS

This poet was an Ionian, perhaps an Athenian, who settled in Sparta. He was contemporary with the second Messenian war (685-668 B.C.), and the victory obtained in that war by the Spartans was due in great measure to his stirring war-songs. His work is in the elegiac metre, with the exception of the two following specimens of marching-songs.

The references for Tyrtaeus are to Bergk's second volume.

I

(15)

Ἄγετ', ὦ Σπάρτας εὐάνδρου
κοῦροι πατέρων πολιατᾶν,
λαιᾷ μὲν ἴτυν προβάλεσθε,
δόρυ δεξιτερᾷ δ' εὐτόλμως,[1]
μὴ φειδόμενοι τᾶς ζωᾶς·
οὐ γὰρ πάτριον τᾷ Σπάρτᾳ.

March, ye sons of sires who are citizens of Sparta rich in heroes, with the left hand bring forward the shield, and with the right the spear, with a good heart, sparing not your lives, for that is not the ancient way of Sparta.

II

(16)

Ἄγετ', ὦ Σπάρτας ἔνοπλοι κοῦροι, ποτὶ τὰν Ἄρεος κίνασιν.

Forward, O arm-bearing sons of Sparta, in the war-god's measure.

---

[1] Bergk's proposed restoration of the line. He prints δόρυ δ' εὐτόλμως [βάλλετε].

ARCHILOCHUS

Archilochus was an Ionian of the island of Paros, and led the wandering life of a fighting adventurer. His *floruit* may be placed between 710-670 B.C. The best-known incident in his private career was the refusal of his fellow-townsman Lycambes to allow him to proceed to marriage with his daughter Neobule, to whom he was already betrothed. The fierce invectives of the poet in iambic verse were said to have driven Lycambes and his daughters to suicide.

The references are to Bergk's second volume.

I
(51)

Ἔα Πάρον καὶ σῦκα κεῖνα καὶ θαλάσσιον βίον.

Let Paros go with its figs and its sea fare.

II
(54)

Γλαῦκ', ὅρα, βαθὺς γὰρ ἤδη κύμασιν ταράσσεται
πόντος, ἀμφὶ δ' ἄκρα Γυρέων ὀρθὸν ἵσταται νέφος,
σῆμα χειμῶνος· κιχάνει δ' ἐξ ἀελπτίης φόβος.

Take heed, Glaucus, for now the deep sea is stirred with waves, and round the tops of the Gyrae a cloud stands sheer, a sign of storm, and terror is at hand unlooked for.

III
(55)

Καὶ νέους θάρσυνε· νίκης δ' ἐν θεοῖσι πείρατα.

And hearten the young warriors, but the issues of victory are with the gods.

IV
(56)

Τοῖς θεοῖς τίθει τὰ πάντα· πολλάκις μὲν ἐκ κακῶν
ἄνδρας ὀρθοῦσιν μελαίνῃ κειμένους ἐπὶ χθονί,
πολλάκις δ' ἀνατρέπουσι καὶ μάλ' εὖ βεβηκότας

ὑπτίους κλίνουσ᾽· ἔπειτα πολλὰ γίγνεται κακά,
καὶ βίου χρήμῃ πλανᾶται καὶ νόου παρήορος.

To the gods assign all things. Often they raise upright from misfortunes men prone upon the dark earth, and often they overturn and lay them low when they have planted themselves right firmly. Then many evils come, and the man wanders in need of sustenance, with mind distraught.

V

(58)

Οὐ φιλέω μέγαν στρατηγὸν οὐδὲ διαπεπλιγμένον,
οὐδὲ βοστρύχοισι γαῦρον οὐδ᾽ ὑπεξυρημένον,
ἀλλά μοι σμικρός τις εἴη καὶ περὶ κνήμας ἰδεῖν
ῥοικός, ἀσφαλέως βεβηκὼς ποσσί, καρδίης πλέος.

I like not a leader big and straddling, proud of his curls and shaven; but let me have one who is little, showing legs that bend inward, standing firm upon his feet, full of courage.

VI

(59)

Quoted by Plutarch in reference to the numbers who claimed a share in the murder of the emperor Galba.

Ἑπτὰ γὰρ νεκρῶν πεσόντων, οὓς ἐμάρψαμεν ποσίν,
χίλιοι φονῆες ἐσμέν.

For though but seven, whom we overtook, fell in death, we the slayers are a thousand.

VII

(63)

Οὔ τις αἰδοῖος μετ' ἀστῶν κἀναρίθμιος θανών
γίγνεται· χάριν δὲ μᾶλλον τοῦ ζοοῦ διώκομεν.

No one when he has died is held in honour and esteem among the citizens, but we turn rather after the excellence of the living man.

VIII

(64)

Οὐ γὰρ ἐσθλὰ κατθανοῦσι κερτομέειν ἐπ' ἀνδράσιν.

For it is not noble to make mock of the dead.

IX

(65)

Ἓν δ' ἐπίσταμαι μέγα,
τὸν κακῶς με δρῶντα δεινοῖς ἀνταμείβεσθαι κακοῖς.

One great thing I know, to requite with stern evils him who does evilly to me.

X

(66)

Θυμέ, θύμ' ἀμηχάνοισι κήδεσιν κυκώμενε,
ἄνεχε,[1] δυσμενῶν δ' ἀλέξευ προσβαλὼν ἐναντίον
στέρνον, ἐν δοκοῖσιν ἐχθρῶν πλησίον κατασταθεὶς
ἀσφαλέως· καὶ μήτε νικῶν ἀμφάδην ἀγάλλεο,

---

[1] Bergk retains the corrupt ἐνάδευ.

μήτε νικηθεὶς ἐν οἴκῳ καταπεσὼν ὀδύρεο,
ἀλλὰ χαρτοῖσίν τε χαῖρε καὶ κακοῖσιν ἀσχάλα
μὴ λίην. γίγνωσκε δ' οἷος ῥυσμὸς ἀνθρώπους ἔχει.

Endure, endure, my soul, disquieted by griefs beyond remedy, and, setting thy breast against the foe, hold thy ground, taking thy stand firm and close amid the spears of the enemy. If thou conquerest, exult not openly; if thou art conquered, lie not down in thy house and mourn. But rejoice in that which is meet for rejoicing, and grieve not over much at calamities, but learn what condition prevails among men.

XI
(69)

Νῦν δὲ Λεώφιλος μὲν ἄρχει, Λεώφιλος δ' ἐπικρατεῖ,
Λεωφίλῳ δὲ πάντα κεῖται, Λεώφιλος δ' ἀκουέτω.

Now Leophilus rules, and Leophilus is master, and upon Leophilus all things depend,—yet let Leophilus give ear.

XII
(70)

Τοῖος ἀνθρώποισι θυμός, Γλαῦκε, Λεπτίνεω παῖ,
γίγνεται θνητοῖς, ὁκοίην Ζεὺς ἐπ' ἡμέρην ἄγῃ,
καὶ φρονεῦσι τοῖ', ὁκοίοις ἐγκυρέωσιν ἔργμασιν.

Such, O Glaucus, son of Leptines, as the day which Zeus brings upon them does the spirit of mortal men become, and such are their thoughts as the deeds upon which they light.

XIII
(71)

Εἰ γὰρ ὡς ἐμοὶ γένοιτο χεῖρα Νεοβούλης θιγεῖν.

O that it might be mine to touch the hand of Neobule.

XIV
(73)

Ἤμβλακον, καὶ πού τιν' ἄλλον ἥδ' ἄτη κιχήσατο.

I sinned, and perchance this madness has overtaken another.

XV
(74)

An Eclipse.

Χρημάτων ἄελπτον οὐδέν ἐστιν οὐδ' ἀπώμοτον,
οὐδὲ θαυμάσιον, ἐπειδὴ Ζεὺς πατὴρ Ὀλυμπίων
ἐκ μεσημβρίης ἔθηκε νύκτ' ἀποκρύψας φάος
ἡλίου λάμποντος· λυγρὸν δ' ἦλθ' ἐπ' ἀνθρώπους
δέος.
ἐκ δὲ τοῦ καὶ πιστὰ πάντα κἀπίελπτα γίγνεται
ἀνδράσιν· μηδεὶς ἔθ' ὑμῶν εἰσορῶν θαυμαζέτω,
μηδ' ὅταν δελφῖσι θῆρες ἀνταμείψωνται νομὸν
ἐνάλιον καί σφιν θαλάσσης ἠχέεντα κύματα
φίλτερ' ἠπείρου γένηται, τοῖσι δ' ὑλήειν[1] ὄρος.

Nothing is to be unlooked for by men, nothing gainsaid upon oath, nothing is marvellous, seeing

---

[1] Bergk's conjecture for ἡδὺ ἦν which he retains in his text.

that Zeus, father of the Olympians, has brought about night from noon-day, hiding the light of the shining sun, and grievous fear came upon men. From that time all things may be believed and expected by man. Let none of you any more wonder at what he sees, not even when the wild beasts take in exchange from the dolphins the pasture of the sea, and the sounding waves of the deep become dearer to them than the land, and the wooded mountain more dear to the dolphins.

XVI
(75)

Κλῦθ' ἄναξ Ἥφαιστε καί μοι σύμμαχος γουνουμένῳ
ἵλαος γενοῦ, χαρίζευ δ' οἷάπερ χαρίζεαι.

Listen, king Hephaestus, and give favouring aid to my prayer, and be gracious with thy wonted grace.

XVII
(77)

Ὡς Διωνύσοι' ἄνακτος καλὸν ἐξάρξαι μέλος
οἶδα διθύραμβον, οἴνῳ συγκεραυνωθεὶς φρένας.

For I know how to start the dithyramb, the goodly strain of sovereign Dionysus, my soul thunder-smitten with wine.

XVIII
(78)

Πολλὸν δὲ πίνων καὶ χαλίκρητον μέθυ,
οὔτε τῖμον εἰσενεγκών . . .
οὐδὲ μὴν κληθεὶς (ὑφ' ἡμῶν) ἦλθες, οἷα δὴ φίλος·
ἀλλά σ' (ἡ) γαστὴρ νόον τε καὶ φρένας παρήγαγεν
εἰς ἀναιδείην.

But you came drinking much unmixed wine, not paying your share, nor invited by us as a friend; but the greed of your belly turned your mind and heart to shamelessness.

XIX
(79)

Ἐρασμονίδη Χαρίλαε, χρῆμά τοι γελοῖον
ἐρέω, πολὺ φίλταθ' ἑταίρων, τέρψεαι δ' ἀκούων.

Charilaus, son of Erasmon, dearest by far of my companions, a mirthful matter will I relate to thee, and thou wilt rejoice hearing it.

XX
(84)

Δύστηνος ἔγκειμαι πόθῳ
ἄψυχος, χαλεπῇσι θεῶν ὀδύνῃσιν ἕκητι
πεπαρμένος δι' ὀστέων.

Hapless I am wrapped in desire, life-bereft, pierced through the marrow with cruel pangs by the will of the gods.

XXI
(85)

'Αλλά μ' ὁ λυσιμελής, ὦ 'ταῖρε, δάμναται πόθος.

But desire, that makes loose the limbs, overcomes me, O friend.

XXII
(86)

This and the two following fragments refer to the fable of the eagle making an alliance with a fox, and then devouring its cubs. Fragment XXIII. is the defiance of the eagle after committing the deed, fragment XXIV. the appeal for justice of the fox. The implied reference is to the treachery of Lycambes.

Αἶνός τις ἀνθρώπων ὅδε,
ὡς ἄρ' ἀλώπηξ καἰετὸς ξυνωνίην
ἔμιξαν.

This tale there is among men, that a fox and eagle made once upon a time a league together.

XXIII
(87)

Ὁρᾷς ἵν' ἔστ' ἐκεῖνος ὑψηλὸς πάγος,
τρηχύς τε καὶ παλίγκοτος,
ἐν τῷ κάθημαι σὴν ἐλαφρίζων μάχην.

Thou seest where is yonder lofty crag, rough and frowning, on which I sit making light of thy warfare.

XXIV

(88)

'Ω Ζεῦ, πάτερ Ζεῦ, σὸν μὲν οὐράνου κράτος,
σὺ δ' ἔργ' ἐπ' ἀνθρώπων ὁρᾷς
λεωργὰ καὶ θεμιστά, σοὶ δὲ θηρίων
ὕβρις τε καὶ δίκη μέλει.

Zeus, father Zeus, thine is the lordship of heaven, and thou beholdest among men deeds heinous and righteous, and to thee the wrong-doing of beasts and its punishment is a care.

XXV

(93)

Τῇ μὲν ὕδωρ ἐφόρει
δολοφρονέουσα χειρί, τῇτέρῃ δὲ πῦρ.

With crafty intent she was bearing in the one hand water, and in the other fire.

XXVI

(94)

Πάτερ Λυκάμβα, ποῖον ἐφράσω τόδε;
τίς σὰς παρήειρε φρένας;
ἧς τὸ πρὶν ἠρήρησθα· νῦν δὲ δὴ πολύς
ἀστοῖσι φαίνεαι γέλως.

Father Lycambes, what thing is this thou hast devised? Who has made thy mind distraught? Once thou wast steadfast therein, but now thou art a great laughing-stock in the eyes of the people.

XXVII
(96)

Addressed to Lycambes.

Ὅρκον δ' ἐνοσφίσθης μέγαν
ἅλας τε καὶ τράπεζαν.

But thou wast false to a great oath, and to the salt and table of hospitality.

XXVIII
(100)

Οὐκέθ' ὁμῶς θάλλεις ἁπαλὸν χρόα· κάρφεται γὰρ
ἤδη.

No longer has thy tender flesh the same bloom, for now it becomes withered.

XXIX
(103)

Τοῖος γὰρ φιλότητος ἔρως ὑπὸ καρδίην ἐλυσθεὶς
πολλὴν κατ' ἀχλὺν ὀμμάτων ἔχευεν,
κλέψας ἐκ στηθέων ἁπαλὰς φρένας.

Such passion of love, winding beneath my heart, shed thick mist over my eyes, stealing the tender soul from my breast.

EUMELUS

Eumelus was one of the ruling family of the Bacchiadae of Corinth, of quite early but uncertain date. The reference in the first line of his fragment is to the Messenian Zeus.

Τῷ γὰρ Ἰθωμάτᾳ καταθύμιος ἔπλετο Μοῖσα
ἁ καθαρὰν (κίθαριν) καὶ ἐλεύθερα σάμβαλ' ἔχοισα.

For dear to the heart of the god of Ithome was the Muse that has the simple lyre and the sandals of freedom.

TERPANDER

A Lesbian by birth, Terpander became, like Tyrtaeus, resident at Sparta. He belongs in date to the earlier half of the seventh century B.C. His innovation in music is referred to in Frag. v.

I

(1)

Ζεῦ πάντων ἀρχά,
πάντων ἀγήτωρ,
Ζεῦ, σοὶ σπένδω
ταύταν ὕμνων ἀρχάν.

Zeus, the beginning of all things, the ruler of all things, Zeus, to thee I make libation of this beginning of song.

II

(2)

To Apollo

Ἀμφί μοι αὖτε ἄναχθ' ἑκαταβόλου
ἀειδέτω φρήν.

Let my spirit sing again of the far-darting king.

III

(3)

Σπένδωμεν ταῖς Μνάμας
παισὶν Μώσαις
καὶ τῷ Μωσάρχῳ
Λατοῦς υἱεῖ.

Let us pour to the Muses, daughters of Memory, and to the lord of the Muses, the son of Leto.

IV

(4)

To the Dioscuri

Ὦ Ζανὸς καὶ Λήδας κάλλιστοι σωτῆρες.

Children of Zeus and Leda, most glorious saviours.

V

(5)

Σοὶ δ' ἡμεῖς τετράγηρυν ἀποστέρξαντες ἀοιδάν
ἑπτατόνῳ φόρμιγγι νέους κελαδήσομεν ὕμνους.

But we, rejecting the four-toned strain, will chant new hymns to thee upon a lyre of seven strings.

VI
(6)
Sparta

Ἔνθ' αἰχμά τε νέων θάλλει καὶ μῶσα λίγεια
καὶ δίκα εὐρυάγυια, καλῶν ἐπιτάρροθος ἔργων.

There the spear of the warrior has power, and the clear-voiced muse, and justice seated in the broad streets, the upholder of righteous deeds.

ALCMAN

Alcman was a native of Sardis who became an adopted citizen of Sparta. His life extends over the greater part of the seventh century B.C. His fragments indicate a freedom and luxury of living unlike the narrower Spartan system of historical times.

I
(1)

Μῶσ' ἄγε, Μῶσα λίγεια πολυμμελὲς
αἰενάοιδε μέλος
νεοχμὸν ἄρχε παρσένοις ἀείδεν.

Muse of the clear voice, ever singing, come, begin a new strain of many notes for the maidens to sing.

II
(6)

A Wave

Χερσόνδε κωφὸν ἐν φύκεσσι πιτνεῖ.

Noiseless it falls to the land amongst the seaweed.

III
(7)

Ἀ Μῶσα κέκλαγ', ἁ λίγεια Σειρήν.

The Muse rings forth, the clear-voiced Siren.

IV
(16)

To Hera

Καὶ τὶν εὔχομαι φέροισα
τόνδ' ἐλιχρύσω πυλεῶνα
κήρατῶ κυπαίρω.

And to thee I make my prayer, bringing this wreath of marigold and goodly sweet gale.

V
(21)

To Aphrodite

Κύπρον ἱμερτὰν λιποῖσα καὶ Πάφον περιρρύταν.

Leaving fair Cyprus and sea-girt Paphos.

VI
(22)

Φοίναις δὲ καὶ ἐν θιάσοισιν
ἀνδρείων παρὰ δαιτυμόνεσσιν
πρέπει παιᾶνα κατάρχειν.

Fitting it is at the banquets and revels of messmates to raise the pæan among the feasters.

VII

(23)

The following are fragments of a Parthenion, or processional hymn of maidens, perhaps, if Bergk's conjecture Ὀρθίᾳ towards the end of the second stanza be right, in honour of Artemis, Orthia being a Spartan epithet of Artemis. Only the more intelligible parts have been here printed. The first words in the text refer to the slaughter of Hippocoon and his sons by the Dioscuri, the poet having taken this as an example of divine vengeance. From that subject he digresses to the praises of Agido, one of the members of his chorus; but the rival charms of Agesichora, the leader of the chorus, distract him. The appeal to the latter to remain seems to indicate that she was on the point of retiring, abashed by the poet's compliments.

... ἄλαστα δὲ
ἔργα πάσον κακὰ μησαμένοι.

ἔστι τις σιῶν τίσις,
ὁ δ' (ὄλβι)ος, ὅστις εὔφρων
ἁμέραν (δι)απλέκει
ἄκλαυστος.[1] ἐγὼν δ' ἀείδω
Ἀγιδῶς τὸ φῶς· ὁρῶ·
ῥ'ὥτ' ἅλιος, ὅνπερ ἅμιν
Ἀγιδὼ μαρτύρεται
φαίνεν· ἐμὲ δ' οὔτ' ἐπαινὲν
οὔτε μωμῆσθαι νιν ἁ κλεννὰ χοραγὸς

[1] Bergk ... κ ... ος.

οὐδὲ λῶσ' ἐῇ· δοκέει γὰρ ἤμεν αὖτα
ἐμπρεπὴς τώς, ὥπερ αἴ τις
ἐν βοτοῖς στάσειεν ἵππον
παγὸν ἀεθλοφόρον καναχάποδα,
νῶμ'[1] ὑποπετριδίων ὀνείρων.

ἦ οὐχ ὁρῇς; ὁ μὲν κέλης
Ἐνετικύς, ἁ δὲ χαίτα
τᾶς ἐμᾶς ἀνεψιᾶς
Ἀγησιχόρας ἐπανθεῖ
χρυσὸς ὣς ἀκήρατος,
τό τ' ἀργύριον πρόσωπον
διαφάδαν — τί τοι λέγω; —
Ἀγησιχόρα, μέν' αὖτα. —
ἁ δὲ δευτέρα πεδ' Ἀγιδὼν τὸ εἶδος
ἵππος εἰβήνῳ Κολαξαῖος δραμεῖται.
ταὶ πελειάδες γὰρ ἁμίν
Ὀρθίᾳ φᾶρος φεροίσαις
νύκτα δἰ ἀμβροσίαν ἄτε σήριον
ἄστρον αὐειρομέναι μάχονται.

Οὔτε γάρ τι πορφύρας
τόσσος κόρος, ὥστ' ἀμύναι,
οὔτε ποικίλος δράκων
παγχρύσιος, οὐδὲ μίτρα
Λυδία νεανίδων
        . . . ἄγαλμα,
οὐδὲ ταὶ Ναννῶς κόμαι,
ἀλλ' οὐδ' Ἐράτα σιειδής,

---

[1] νῶμα = νόημα, Bergk's conjecture. In his text he leaves a lacuna.

οὐδὲ Συλακίς τε καὶ Κλεησισήρα,
οὐδ' ἐς Αἰνησιμβρότας ἐνθοῖσα, φασεῖς·
Ἀσταφίς τέ μοι γένοιτο
καὶ ποτηνέποι Φιλύλλα,
Δαμαγόρα τ' ἐρατά τε Ἰανθεμίς,
ἀλλ' Ἀγησιχόρα με τηρεῖ.

But for the shameful deeds they had devised they suffered an evil fate. There is a vengeance exacted by the gods, and he is blest whoso brings the day to a close in gladness, without tears. For me I sing the radiance of Agido; like the sun she speeds, and bears witness to us that he is shining. But the fair leader of the chorus, though she were willing, suffers me not either to praise or to blame Agido; for it is she, she that shows herself conspicuous, as though one should place among herds of cattle a sturdy prize-winning horse, with ringing hoofs, such as is imaged in winged dreams.

See you not? 'Tis a steed of Enetian race, and the locks of my kinswoman Agesichora are bright as pure gold, and her face of silver sheen is manifestly—what should I liken it to?—Nay, keep thy place, Agesichora.—But next in beauty to Agido she will run with her like a horse of Kolaxis with the hound; for these doves vie one with another, rising before us through the divine night like the star of Sirius, as we bear the robe to Artemis.

Here is no such wealth of purple as to give a

change of raiment, nor cunningly-wrought, snake-shaped bracelet all of gold, nor Lydian snood, the ornament of maidens, nor is Nanno of the braided tresses with us, nor yet goddess-like Erate, nor Sylacis and Cleesisera; nor will you go to the house of Aenesimbrota and say, 'O that Astaphis were my companion, and that Philylla held speech with me, and Damagora, and fair Ianthemis'; not these, but Agesichora protects me.

VIII
(24)
Alcman Described

Οὐκ εἷς ἀνὴρ ἄγροικος οὐδὲ
σκαιὸς οὐδὲ παρὰ σοφοῖσιν
οὐδὲ Θεσσαλὸς γένος
οὐδ' Ἐρυσιχαῖος οὐδὲ ποιμήν,
ἀλλὰ Σαρδίων ἀπ' ἀκρᾶν.

Thou art not a man clownish, nor dull-witted, not even in the eyes of the wise, nor a Thessalian in race, nor from Erysiche, nor a shepherd, but from lofty Sardis.

IX
(24)

Ἔπη τάδε καὶ μέλος Ἀλκμάν
εὗρε, γεγλωσσαμένον
κακκαβίδων στόμα συνθέμενος.

These words and strains Alcman found by heeding the note-giving mouth of the partridge.

X
(26)

Οὔ μ' ἔτι, παρθενικαὶ μελιγάρυες ἱμερόφωνοι,
γυῖα φέρειν δύναται· βάλε δὴ βάλε κηρύλος εἴην,
ὅς τ' ἐπὶ κύματος ἄνθος ἅμ' ἀλκυόνεσσι ποτῆται
νηλεγὲς ἦτορ ἔχων, ἁλιπόρφυρος εἴαρος ὄρνις.

No longer, O soft - voiced, sweetly - speaking maidens, can my limbs bear me. Would, ah! would that I were the halcyon that flies with its mates[1] over the surface of the wave, keeping an untroubled heart, the sea-blue bird of spring.

XI
(28)

Δῦσαν δ' ἄπρακτα νεάνιδες, ὥστ'
ὄρνεις ἱέρακος ὑπερπταμένῳ.

And the maidens sank helpless, like birds when a kite flies overhead.

XII
(33)

Καί ποκά τοι δώσω τρίποδος κύτος,
ᾧ κ' ἔνι . . . ἀγείραις·
ἀλλ' ἔτι νῦν γ' ἄπυρος, τάχα δὲ πλέος
ἔτνεος, οἷον ὁ παμφάγος Ἀλκμάν
ἠράσθη χλιερὸν πεδὰ τὰς τροπάς·

---

[1] The she-halcyons were believed to support the male, when it had become old, upon their wings.

οὔτι γὰρ ἠῢ τετυγμένον ἔσθει,
ἀλλὰ τὰ κοινὰ γάρ, ὥσπερ ὁ δᾶμος,
ζατεύει.

And I will give you at some time a hollow cauldron in which to bring together . . . Now it is still untouched by fire, but soon it will be full of pea-soup, such as Alcman the all-devouring loves warm after mid-winter. For he eats nothing daintily prepared, but seeks after common things, like the people.

XIII

(34)

A Maenad

Πολλάκι δ' ἐν κορυφαῖς ὀρέων, ὅκα
θεοῖσιν ἄδῃ πολύφαμος ἑορτά,
χρύσιον ἄγγος ἔχοισα μέγαν σκύφον,
οἷα τε ποιμένες ἄνδρες ἔχουσιν,
χερσὶ λεόντειον γάλα θήσαο,
τυρὸν ἐτύρησας μέγαν ἄτρυφον ἀργιφόνταν.

And often on the heights of the mountains, when the many-voiced festal rites delight the gods, bearing a golden pail, a great bowl, such as shepherds have, thou didst press forth with thy hands the milk of a lioness, thou didst make a cheese huge, unbroken, shining white.

XIV

(35)

Sparta

Ἕρπει γὰρ ἄντα τῷ σιδάρῳ
τὸ καλῶς κιθαρίσδην.

For the skilful playing of the lyre has equal rank with the sword.

XV

(36)

Ἔρος με δαῦτε Κύπριδος Ϝέκατι
γλυκὺς κατείβων καρδίαν ἰαίνει.

Again does Love, streaming sweetly down at the bidding of the Cyprian goddess, make warm my heart.

XVI

(37)

A Poetess

Τοῦτο Ϝαδείαν . . . Μωσᾶν ἔδειξεν
δῶρον μάκαιρα παρθένων
ἁ ξανθὰ Μεγαλοστράτα.

This gift of the sweet Muses golden-haired Megalostrate, queen amongst maidens, has given to our sight.

XVII
(38)

Ἀφροδίτα μὲν οὐκ ἔστι, μάργος δ' Ἔρως οἷα παῖς
παίσδει
ἄκρ' ἐπ' ἄνθη καβαίνων, ἃ μή μοι θίγῃς, τῶ κυ-
παιρίσκω.

Not here is Aphrodite, but mad love wantons like a boy, treading the topmost flowers of the sweet gale, which, prithee, touch not.

XVIII
(40)

Δύσπαρις, αἰνόπαρις, κακὸν Ἑλλάδι βωτιανείρᾳ.

Paris of ill omen, fatal Paris, bane of hero-nurturing Hellas.

XIX
(42)

Τίς δ' ἄν, τίς ποκα ῥᾳ̈ ἄλλω νόον ἀνδρὸς ἐνίσποι;

But who would ever easily declare the mind of another?

XX
(43)

Καὶ ποικίλον ἶκα, τὸν ἀμπέλων
ὀφθαλμῶν ὀλετῆρα.

And the spotted worm, destroyer of the vine-buds.

XXI

(45)

Μῶσ' ἄγε, Καλλιόπα, θύγατερ Διός,
ἄρχ' ἐρατῶν ἐπέων, ἐπὶ δ' ἵμερον
ὕμνῳ καὶ χαρίεντα τίθει χορόν.

Come, O Muse Calliope, daughter of Zeus, begin the goodly lay, and add desire to the song, and a fair band of dancers.

XXII

(47)

Εἴπατέ μοι τάδε, φῦλα βροτήσια.

Tell me this, ye tribes of mortals.

XXIII

(48)

Οἷα Διὸς θυγάτηρ
ἔρσα τρέφει καὶ Σελάνας [δίας].

Such things as the dew nourishes, daughter of the air and moon.

XXIV

(50)

Μέγα γείτονι γείτων.

Neighbour to neighbour is a great good.

XXV

(57)

Μηδέ μ' ἀείδην ἀπέρυκε.

And keep me not from singing.

XXVI

(58)

Ῥιπᾶν ὄρος ἀνθέων ὕλᾳ,
Νυκτὸς μελαίνας στέρνον.

The Rhipaean heights clothed with forest, the bosom of black Night.

XXVII

(60)

Εὕδουσιν δ' ὀρέων κορυφαί τε καὶ φάραγγες,
πρώονές τε καὶ χαράδραι,
φύλλα θ' ἑρπετά θ' ὅσσα τρέφει μέλαινα γαῖα,
θῆρες τ' ὀρεσκῷοι καὶ γένος μελισσᾶν
καὶ κνώδαλ' ἐν βένθεσι πορφυρέας ἁλός·
εὕδουσιν δ' οἰωνῶν
φῦλα τανυπτερύγων.

The crests and hollows of the mountains are asleep, and the headlands and ravines, and the leaves, and all creeping things that the dark earth nourishes, and the mountain-haunting beasts, and the race of bees, and the creatures in the depths of the dark-gleaming ocean; and there is sleep among the tribes of broad-winged birds.

XXVIII
(66)

Ὅσαι δὲ παίδες ἀμέων
ἐντί, τὸν κιθαριστὰν αἰνέοντι.

All the girls in our band praise the poet singing to his lyre.

XXIX
(67)

Οἶδα δ' ὀρνίχων νόμως
πάντων.

And I know the songs of all birds.

XXX
(76)

Ὥρας δ' ἔσηκε τρεῖς, θέρος
καὶ χεῖμα κὠπώραν τρίταν,
καὶ τέτρατον τὸ Fῆρ, ὅκα
σάλλει μέν, ἐσθίεν δ' ἅδαν
οὐκ ἔστιν.

And he made three seasons, summer, winter, and autumn the third, and spring for the fourth, when the world is in bloom, and one cannot satisfy desire in eating.

XXXI
(81)

Fate

Λεπτὰ δ' ἄταρπος, νηλεὴς δ' ἀνάγκα.

Narrow is the path and pitiless the doom.

XXXII

(87)

Tantalus

Ἀνὴρ δ' ἐν ἁρμένοισιν
ἀλιτρὸς ἦστ' ἐπὶ θάκω κατὰ πέτρας
ὁρέων μὲν οὐδέν, δοκέοντι δ' (ἐοικώς).

But he, the transgressor, sat upon a couch in the midst of good cheer, a stone overhanging him, seeing nought, but like to one who thinks he sees.

ARION

Arion, by birth a native of Lesbos, lived in Corinth under the protection of the tyrant Periander, who held power from 625-585 B.C. He was the first to organise the dithyramb, or choral hymn to Dionysus. His poetical fame is evidenced by the story of his preservation by the dolphins. The following poem, however, is generally considered from its diffuseness, and from other internal evidence, to be the work of some later poet of the dithyrambic school.

"Ύψιστε θεῶν,
πόντιε χρυσοτρίαινα, Πόσειδον,
γαιάοχ', ἐγκύμον' ἀν' ἅλμαν·
βραγχίοις περὶ δὲ σὲ πλωτοί
θῆρες χορεύουσι κύκλῳ,
κούφοισι ποδῶν ῥίμμασιν
ἐλάφρ' ἀναπαλλόμενοι, σιμοί,
φριξαύχενες, ὠκύδρομοι σκύλακες, φιλόμουσοι
δελφῖνες, ἔναλα θρέμματα
κουρᾶν Νηρεΐδων θεᾶν,
ἃς ἐγείνατ' Ἀμφιτρίτα·
οἵ μ' εἰς Πέλοπος γᾶν ἐπὶ Ταιναρίαν ἀκτάν
ἐπορεύσατε πλαζόμενον Σικελῷ ἐνὶ πόντῳ,
κυρτοῖσι νώτοις ὀχέοντες,
ἄλοκα Νηρεΐας πλακός
τέμνοντες, ἀστιβῆ πόρον, φῶτες δόλιοι
ὥς μ' ἀφ' ἁλιπλόου γλαφυρᾶς νεώς
εἰς οἶδμα πορφυροῦν λίμνας ἔριψαν.

Poseidon of the golden trident, lord of the sea, mightiest of gods, earth-encircling, dweller in the teeming brine, around thee fin-borne creatures gambol in a circle, the music-loving dolphins, leaping nimbly up with light-darting feet, snub-nosed and with bristling manes, whelps swift of speed, the sea-brood of the divine Nereid maids whom Amphitrite bore:—ye who, when treacherous men cast me from the hollow, sea-voyaging ship into the dark billows of the deep, brought me, adrift on the Sicilian waters, to the land of Pelops and the headland of Taenarus, carrying me on your curved backs, cleaving the furrow of the ocean plain, a path untrodden.

SAPPHO

Sappho, the greatest woman-poet of antiquity, was born in Lesbos towards the end of the seventh century B.C. She was of aristocratic birth, and the centre of a highly cultivated circle of Lesbian ladies, some of whom stood to her in the relation of pupils. She married, and had one daughter. The story of her hopeless love for Phaon, and her suicide by leaping from the Leucadian rock, is probably a mere fable suggested by the passionate nature of her verse. The name of Phaon does not occur in her extant fragments.

I

∨ (1)

Ποικιλόθρον' ἀθάνατ' 'Αφρόδιτα,
παῖ Δίος, δολόπλοκε, λίσσομαί σε,
μή μ' ἄσαισι μήτ' ὀνίαισι δάμνα,
  πότνια, θῦμον·
ἀλλὰ τυῖδ' ἔλθ', αἴποτε κἀτέρωτα
τᾶς ἔμας αὔδως ἀΐοισα πήλυι
ἔκλυες, πάτρος δὲ δόμον λίποισα
  χρύσιον ἦλθες
ἄρμ' ὑπαζεύξαισα· κάλοι δέ σ' ἆγον
ὤκεες στροῦθοι περὶ γᾶς μελαίνας
πύκνα δινεῦντες πτέρ' ἀπ' ὠράνω αἴθε-
  ρος διὰ μέσσω.
αἶψα δ' ἐξίκοντο· τὺ δ', ὦ μάκαιρα,
μειδιάσαισ' ἀθανάτῳ προσώπῳ,
ἤρε', ὄττι δηὖτε πέπονθα κὤττι
  δηὖτε κάλημι,
κὤττι μοι μάλιστα θέλω γένεσθαι
μαινόλᾳ θύμῳ· τίνα δηὖτε Πείθω
μαῖς ἄγην ἐς σὰν φιλότατα, τίς σ', ὦ
  Ψάπφ', ἀδικήει;
καὶ γὰρ αἰ φεύγει, ταχέως διώξει,
αἰ δὲ δῶρα μὴ δέκετ', ἀλλὰ δώσει,
αἰ δὲ μὴ φίλει, ταχέως φιλήσει
  κωὔκ ἐθέλοισα.

ἔλθε μοι καὶ νῦν, χαλεπᾶν δὲ λῦσον
ἐκ μεριμνᾶν, ὅσσα δέ μοι τέλεσσαι
θῦμος ἰμέρρει, τέλεσον· σὺ δ' αὖτα
σύμμαχος ἔσσο.

Deathless Aphrodite of fair carven throne, guile-weaving daughter of Zeus, I entreat thee, oppress not my heart, O mistress, with grief and torments. But come hither, if ever even at any other time, hearing my voice afar off, thou didst give ear, and didst come, leaving thy father's golden house, having yoked thy chariot. And swiftly above the dark earth the beauteous sparrows, fluttering their feathered wings, bore thee from the sky through mid-air, and quickly they reached their goal. And thou, O goddess, smiling with immortal face, didst ask what has again befallen me, and why I again call, and what in my frenzied heart I most wish to come to pass. 'Whom art thou fain that Persuasion should bring again to thy love? Who does thee wrong, Sappho? For even if she flies, she shall soon pursue, and if she receives not gifts, yet she shall give them, and if she loves not, soon she shall love even against her will.' Now too, I pray thee, come, and free me from bitter cares, and all that my heart yearns to accomplish, do thou accomplish, and be thou thyself my ally.

✗ (2)

Φαίνεταί μοι κῆνος ἴσος θέοισιν
ἔμμεν ὤνηρ, ὄστις ἐναντίος τοι
ἰζάνει, καὶ πλασίον ἆδυ φωνεύ-
 σας ὑπακούει
καὶ γελαίσας ἰμερόεν, τό μοι μὰν
καρδίαν ἐν στήθεσιν ἐπτόασεν·
ὡς γὰρ εὔιδον βροχέως σε, φώνας
 οὐδὲν ἔτ᾽ εἴκει·
ἀλλὰ καμ μὲν γλῶσσα ἔαγε, λέπτον δ᾽
αὔτικα χρῷ πῦρ ὑποδεδρόμακεν,
ὀππάτεσσι δ᾽ οὐδὲν ὄρημ᾽, ἐπιρρόμ-
 βεισι δ᾽ ἄκουαι.
ἀ δὲ μίδρως κακχέεται, τρόμος δὲ
παῖσαν ἄγρει, χλωροτέρα δὲ ποίας
ἔμμι, τεθνάκην δ᾽ ὀλίγω 'πιδεύης
 φαίνομαι (ἄλλα).
ἀλλὰ πὰν τόλματον.

That man seems to me to be the peer of the gods, whosoever sits opposite to thee, and hears close at hand thy soft voice and sweet laughter, which makes, I trow, the heart flutter in my breast. For when I have beheld thee for a little, no longer does any speech come to me, but my tongue is broken, and at once a light fire runs beneath my skin, and I see nothing with my eyes, and there is a ringing in my ears. The sweat pours down, and a trembling seizes all my body, and I am paler than grass, and seem, frenzy-smitten, but a little way from death. Yet must all be dared.

III

(3)

Ἀστερες μὲν ἀμφὶ κάλαν σελάνναν
αἶψ' ἀποκρύπτοισι φάεννον εἶδος,
ὅπποτα πλήθοισα μάλιστα λάμπῃ
    γᾶν . . .
. . . ἀργυρία.

The stars about the fair moon quickly hide their shining face, whenever, drawing nigh, she most illumines the earth with silver light.

IV

(4)

Ἀμφὶ δὲ ψῦχρον κελάδει δι' ὔσδων
μαλίνων, αἰθυσσομένων δὲ φύλλων
    κῶμα καταρρεῖ.

And round the cool water the breeze murmurs through the apple boughs, and slumber streams down from the quivering leaves.

v
(5)

Ἔλθε Κύπρι
χρυσίαισιν ἐν κυλίκεσσιν ἄβρως
συμμεμιγμένον θαλίαισι νέκταρ
οἰνοχεῦσα.

Come, Cypris, pouring in golden cups nectar delicately mingled with delight.

vi
(9)

Αἴθ' ἔγω, χρυσοστέφαν' Ἀφροδίτα,
τόνδε τὸν πάλον λαχόην.

Would that I, O golden-crowned Aphrodite, might win this cast.

vii
(10)
The Muses

Αἴ με τιμίαν ἐπόησαν ἔργα
τὰ σφὰ δοῦσαι.

They made me honoured, giving me their own arts.

viii
(18)

Τάδε νῦν ἑταίραις
ταῖς ἔμαισι τέρπνα κάλως ἀείσω.

Now to my girl-comrades will I sweetly sing these strains of delight.

IX
(12)

Ὄττινας γάρ
εὖ θέω, κῆνοί με μάλιστα σίννον-
ται.

For those most injure me to whom I do well.

X
(14)

Ταῖς κάλαις ὔμμιν (τὸ) νόημα τὦμον
οὐ διάμειπτον.

To you, fair maids, my mind changes not.

XI
(16)

The reference is to doves.

Ταῦσι (δὲ) ψῦχρος μὲν ἔγεντο θῦμος,
παρ δ' ἴεισι τὰ πτέρα.

Their heart grew cold, and they droop their wings.

XII
(19)

Πόδας δέ
ποίκιλος μάσλης ἐκάλυπτε, Λύδιον κάλον ἔργον.

And richly dyed leather, the fair work of Lydia, hid her feet.

XIII

(21)

... Ἔμεθεν δ' ἔχεισθα λάθαν.

But of me thou hast forgetfulness.

XIV

(22)

Ἤ τιν' ἄλλον
(μᾶλλον) ἀνθρώπων ἔμεθεν φίλησθα.

Or thou lovest some other of mortals rather han me.

XV

(23)

Καὶ ποθήω καὶ μάομαι.

I do both yearn and desire.

XVI

(27)

Σκιδναμένας ἐν στήθεσιν ὄργας
μαψυλάκαν γλῶσσαν πεφύλαχθαι.

When anger over-spreads the heart, keep guard on the idly-barking tongue.

XVII

(28)

The answer to Alcaeus (*vid.* Alcaeus, Frag. xxix.), written in his own metre.

Αἰ δ' ἦχες ἔσλων ἴμερον ἢ κάλων,
καὶ μή τι Ϝείπην γλῶσσ' ἐκύκα κάκον,
αἴδως κέ σ' οὐ κίχανεν ὄππατ',
ἀλλ' ἔλεγες περὶ τῶ δικαίως.

If thou hadst a desire for things good and right, and if thy tongue were not planning to speak something ill, shame would not hold down thy eyes, but thou wouldst speak thereon openly.

XVIII

(28)

Στᾶθι κἄντα φίλος . . .
καὶ τὰν ἐπ' ὄσσοις ἀμπέτασον χάριν.

Stand opposite, beloved, and reveal the grace that is upon thine eyes.

XIX

(32)

Μνάσεσθαί τινά φαμι καὶ ὔστερον ἄμμεων.

I say that even hereafter men will remember me.

XX

(33)

Ἤραμαν μὲν ἔγω σέθεν, Ἄτθι, πάλαι πότα.

I loved thee once, Atthis, long ago.

XXI

(34)

Σμίκρα μοι πάϊς ἔμμεν ἐφαίνεο κἄχαρις.

Thou didst seem to me to be a girl small and ngraceful.

XXII

(36)

Οὐκ οἶδ' ὄττι θέω· δύο μοι τὰ νοήματα.

I know not what I should do, my thoughts are vain.

XXIII

(37)

Ψαύην δ' οὐ δοκίμοιμ' ὀράνω δύσι πάχεσιν.

But I deem not that I touch the heavens with ιy two arms.

XXIV

(38)

Ὠς δὲ παῖς πεδὰ μάτερα πεπτερύγωμαι.

And I flutter like a child to its mother.

XXV
(39)

Ἦρος ἄγγελος ἰμερόφωνος ἀήδων.

The messenger of spring, the sweet-voiced nightingale.

XXVI
(40)

Ἔρος δαῦτέ μ' ὁ λυσιμέλης δόνει,
γλυκύπικρον ἀμάχανον ὄρπετον.

Again does love shake me, love that makes loose the limbs, the creature bitter-sweet, resistless.

XXVII
(41)

Ἄτθι, σοὶ δ' ἔμεθεν μὲν ἀπήχθετο
φροντίσδην, ἐπὶ δ' Ἀνδρομέδαν πότῃ.

To thee, Atthis, it was hateful to have thought for me, but thou fliest to Andromeda.

XXVIII
(42)

(Ἔρος δαῦτ' ἐτίναξεν ἔμοι φρένας),
ἄνεμος κατ' ὄρος δρύσιν ἐμπέτων.

Love again stirs my heart, like a wind falling on the oaks upon the mountain.

XX
(33)

'Ηράμαν μὲν ἔγω σέθεν, "Ατθι, πάλαι πότα.

I loved thee once, Atthis, long ago.

XXI
(34)

Σμίκρα μοι πάϊς ἔμμεν ἐφαίνεο κἄχαρις.

Thou didst seem to me to be a girl small and ngraceful.

XXII
(36)

Οὐκ οἶδ' ὅττι θέω· δύο μοι τὰ νοήματα.

I know not what I should do, my thoughts are vain.

XXIII
(37)

Ψαύην δ' οὐ δοκίμοιμ' ὀράνω δύσι πάχεσιν.

But I deem not that I touch the heavens with ιy two arms.

XXIV
(38)

Ὠς δὲ παῖς πεδὰ μάτερα πεπτερύγωμαι.

And I flutter like a child to its mother.

XXV

(39)

Ἦρος ἄγγελος ἰμερόφωνος ἀήδων.

The messenger of spring, the sweet-voiced nightingale.

XXVI

(40)

Ἔρος δαῦτέ μ' ὁ λυσιμέλης δόνει,
γλυκύπικρον ἀμάχανον ὄρπετον.

Again does love shake me, love that makes loose the limbs, the creature bitter-sweet, resistless.

XXVII

(41)

Ἄτθι, σοὶ δ' ἔμεθεν μὲν ἀπήχθετο
φροντίσδην, ἐπὶ δ' Ἀνδρομέδαν πότῃ.

To thee, Atthis, it was hateful to have thought for me, but thou fliest to Andromeda.

XXVIII

(42)

(Ἔρος δαῦτ' ἐτίναξεν ἔμοι φρένας),
ἄνεμος κατ' ὄρος δρύσιν ἐμπέτων.

Love again stirs my heart, like a wind falling on the oaks upon the mountain.

XXIX

(45)

Ἄγε δὴ χέλυ δῖά μοι
φωνάεσσα γένοιο.

Come, divine lyre, make thyself vocal for me.

XXX

(46)

Κἀπάλαις ὑποθύμιδας
πλέκταις ἀμπ' ἀπάλᾳ δέρᾳ.

And soft garlands woven about the soft neck.

XXXI

(51)

Κῆ δ' ἀμβροσίας μὲν κράτηρ ἐκέκρατο,
Ἑρμᾶς δ' ἔλεν ὄλπιν θεοῖς οἰνοχόησαι.
κῆνοι δ' ἄρα πάντες καρχήσιά τ' ἦχον
κἄλειβον, ἀράσαντο δὲ πάμπαν ἔσλα
τῷ γάμβρῳ.

And there a bowl of ambrosia had been mixed, and Hermes took a beaker to pour for the gods. And they all had cups, and made libation, and prayed for the bridegroom all good things.

XXXII

(52)

Δέδυκε μὲν ἁ σελάννα
καὶ Πληΐαδες, μέσαι δέ
νύκτες, παρὰ δ' ἔρχετ' ὤρα,
ἔγω δὲ μόνα κατεύδω.

The moon has set, and the Pleiads, and it is midnight, and the hour goes by, but I lie alone.

XXXIII

(53)

Πλήρης μὲν ἐφαίνετ' ἁ σελάννα,
αἱ δ' ὡς περὶ βῶμον ἐστάθησαν.

The moon showed full, and the women stood as though round an altar.

XXXIV

(54)

Κρῆσσαι νύ ποτ' ὦδ' ἐμμελέως πόδεσσιν
ὠρχεῦντ' ἀπάλοις ἀμφ' ἐρόεντα βῶμον,
πόας τέρεν ἄνθος μάλακον μάτεισαι.

Thus did Cretan maids once dance in time with soft feet round the fair altar, treading the tender yielding blooms of the grass.

XXXV

(56)

Φαῖσι δή ποτα Λήδαν ὑακίνθινον
πεπυκαδμένον ὤιον
εὔρην.

They say that Leda once found a hidden egg, hyacinth-white.

XXXVI

(57)

Ὀφθάλμοις δὲ μέλαις νύκτος ἄωρος.

And upon the eyes the black sleep of night.

XXXVII

(60)

Δεῦτέ νυν ἄβραι Χάριτες, καλλίκομοί τε Μοῖσαι.

Hither now, ye delicate Graces and fair-haired Muses.

XXXVIII

(62)

Κατθνάσκει, Κυθέρη', ἄβρος Ἄδωνις, τί κε θεῖμεν;
καττύπτεσθε κόραι καὶ κατερείκεσθε χίτωνας.

Delicate Adonis is dying, Cytherea, what should we do? Beat upon your breasts, maidens, and rend your garments.

XXXIX

(64)

Love

Ἐλθοντ' ἐξ ὀράνω πορφυρίαν περθέμενον χλάμυν.

Coming from on high, clad in a purple stole.

XL

(65)

Βροδοπάχεες ἄγναι Χάριτες, δεῦτε Δίος κόραι.

Rosy-armed, maiden Graces, daughters of Zeus, come hither.

XLI

(68)

In Mulierem Indoctam

Κατθάνοισα δὲ κείσεαι πότα, κωὐ μναμοσύνα σέθεν
ἔσσετ' οὔτε τότ' οὔτ' ὔστερον· οὐ γὰρ πεδέχεις βρόδων
τῶν ἐκ Πιερίας, ἀλλ' ἀφάνης κἠν Ἀΐδα δόμοις
φοιτάσεις πεδ' ἀμαύρων νεκύων ἐκπεποταμένα.

Some day thou shalt lie low in death, and there shall be no memory of thee neither then nor afterwards, for thou hast no share in the roses from Pieria; but even in the halls of Hades thou shalt wander obscure, flitting with the shadowy dead.

XLII
(69)

Οὐδ' ἴαν δοκίμοιμι προσίδοισαν φάος ἀλίω
ἔσσεσθαι σοφίαν πάρθενον εἰς οὐδένα πω χρόνον
τοιαύταν.

Methinks that in no time to come will any maiden that sees the light of the sun be such in wisdom.

XLIII
(70)

Τίς δ' ἀγροιῶτίς τοι θέλγει νόον,
οὐκ ἐπισταμένα τὰ βράκε' ἕλκην ἐπὶ τῶν σφύρων;

What graceless creature bewitches thy mind, that knows not how to draw her gown about her ankles?

XLIV
(72)

... Ἀλλά τις οὐκ ἔμμι παλιγκότων
ὄργαν, ἀλλ' ἀβάκην τὰν φρέν' ἔχω.

Nay, I am not one of the vindictive in spirit, but have a gentle heart.

XLV
(73)

Αὐτὰρ ὁραῖαι στεφανηπλόκευν.

But in their time they plaited garlands.

XLVI
(75)

'Αλλ' ἔων φίλος ἄμμιν (ἄλλο)
λέχος ἄρνισο νεώτερον·
οὐ γὰρ τλάσομ' ἔγω ξυνοίκην
νέῳ γ' ἔσσα γεραιτέρα.

Be to me a friend, but choose another younger consort, for I thy elder will not endure to mate with a youth.

XLVII
(77)

'Ασαροτέρας οὔδαμ' ἐπ', ὦ 'ραννα, σέθεν τύχοισα.

Having never yet, O fair one, found a maiden more disdainful than thee.

XLVIII
(78)

Σὺ δὲ στεφάνοις, ὦ Δίκα, περθέσθ' ἐράταις φόβαισιν,
ὄρπακας ἀνήτοιο συνέρραισ' ἀπάλαισι χέρσιν·
εὐάνθεσιν ἐκ γὰρ πέλεται καὶ χάριτος μακαιρᾶν
μᾶλλον προτέρην· ἀστεφανώτοισι δ' ἀπυστρέφονται.

But do thou, Dice, place garlands about thy fair tresses, twining sprays of dill with thy tender hands. For to those decked with flowers it is also granted to excel more in the favour of the gods, but from the ungarlanded they turn away.

XLIX
(79)

Ἐγω δὲ φίλημ' ἀβροσύναν, καί μοι ... τὸ λάμπρον
ἔρος ... ἀελίω καὶ τὸ κάλον λέλογχεν.

But I am a lover of daintiness, and my joy in the light of the sun holds within it things radiant and fair.

L
(80)

Ὁ πλοῦτος ἄνευ σεῦ γ' ἀρέτα 'στ' οὐκ ἀσίνης
πάροικος.

Wealth without thee, O virtue, is a mischievous neighbour.

LI
(83)

Δαύοις ἀπάλας ἐτάρας
ἐν στήθεσιν.

Mayest thou sleep in the bosom of thy tender love.

LII
(85)

Εστι μοι κάλα πάϊς, χρυσίοισιν ἀνθέμοισιν
ἐμφέρην ἔχοισα μόρφαν, Κλῆϊς ἀγαπάτα,
ἀντὶ τᾶς ἔγω οὐδὲ Λυδίαν παῖσαν οὐδ' ἔρανναν ...

I have a fair daughter, Cleïs the beloved, in aspect like a golden flower, for whom I would not take all Lydia or beauteous ...

LIII
(90)

Γλύκεια μᾶτερ, οὔτοι δύναμαι κρέκην τὸν ἴστον,
πόθῳ δάμεισα παῖδος βραδίναν δι' Ἀφρόδιταν.

Sweet mother, I cannot weave the web, for I am overcome with love for a youth at the will of delicate Aphrodite.

LIV
(91)

Ἴψοι δὴ τὸ μέλαθρον
  Ὑμήναον
ἀέρρετε τέκτονες ἄνδρες·
  Ὑμήναον.
γάμβρος ἔρχεται ἶσος Ἄρευϊ,
  (Ὑμήναον)
ἄνδρος μεγάλω πόλυ μείζων
  (Ὑμήναον).

Raise the roof high, carpenters (Hymenaeus!). The bridegroom comes, mighty as Ares, (Hymenaeus!), taller far than a tall man, (Hymenaeus!).

LV
(92)

Πέρροχος, ὡς ὅτ' ἄοιδος ὁ Λέσβιος ἀλλοδάποισιν.

Towering as the Lesbian singer above those of other lands.

LVI
(93)
The Bride

Οἶον τὸ γλυκύμαλον ἐρεύθεται ἄκρῳ ἐπ᾽ ἴσδῳ
ἄκρον ἐπ᾽ ἀκροτάτῳ· λελάθοντο δὲ μαλοδρόπηες,
οὐ μὰν ἐκλελάθοντ᾽, ἀλλ᾽ οὐκ ἐδύναντ᾽ ἐπίκεσθαι.

Like the sweet apple which reddens upon the top bough, at the top of the topmost bough, but the gatherers forgot it, nay, forgot it not utterly, but could not reach it.

LVII
(94)
Unwooed

Οἴαν τὰν ὑάκινθον ἐν οὔρεσι ποίμενες ἄνδρες
πόσσι καταστείβοισι, χάμαι δ᾽ ἐπιπορφύρει ἄνθος.

Like the hyacinth which the shepherds tread underfoot upon the mountains, and its flower lies purple on the ground.

LVIII
(95)
The Marriage Star

Ϝέσπερε, πάντα φέρων, ὄσα φαίνολις ἐσκέδασ᾽ αὔως,
φέρεις οἶν, φέρεις αἶγα, φέρεις ἄπυ ματέρι παῖδα.

Hesperus, bringing all things that the bright dawn scattered, thou bringest the sheep and the goat, thou hurriest the child to its mother.

LIX
(98)

Possibly taunts directed by the maidens against the bridegroom's friend who kept guard over the marriage chamber.

Θυρώρῳ πόδες ἐπτορόγυιοι,
τὰ δὲ σάμβαλα πεμπεβόηα,
πίσυγγοι δὲ δέκ' ἐξεπόνασαν.

Seven fathoms long are the door-keeper's feet, and his shoes are of five bulls' hides, and ten shoemakers wrought them.

LX
(99)

Ολβιε γάμβρε σοὶ μὲν δὴ γάμος, ὡς ἄραο,
ἐκτετέλεστ', ἔχης δὲ πάρθενον, ἂν ἄραο.

Happy bridegroom, for thee has marriage come to pass as thou didst pray, and thou hast the maiden for whom thou didst pray.

LXI
(101)

Ὁ μὲν γὰρ κάλος, ὅσσον ἴδην, πέλεται (ἄγαθος),
ὁ δε κἄγαθος αὔτικα καὶ κάλος ἔσσεται.

For he that is beautiful is good so far as to look upon, but he that is good will forthwith be beautiful as well.

LXII
(104)

Τίῳ σ', ὦ φίλε γάμβρε, κάλως ἐϊκάσδω;
ὄρπακι βραδίνῳ σε κάλιστ' ἐϊκάσδω.

To what, dear bridegroom, should I rightly liken thee? To a slender sapling do I most rightly liken thee.

LXIII
(105)

Χαῖρε, νύμφα,
χαῖρε, τίμιε γάμβρε, πόλλα.

Hail, O bride, much hail, O honoured bridegroom.

LXIV
(106)

Οὐ γὰρ ἦν ἀτέρα πάϊς, ὦ γάμβρε, τοιαύτα.

For no other girl, O bridegroom, was like this.

LXV
(109)

Παρθενία, παρθενία, ποῖ με λίποισ' ἀποίχῃ;
Οὐκέτι ἤξω πρὸς σέ, οὐκέτι ἤξω.

Maidenhood, maidenhood, whither hast thou gone leaving me?
Never more will I come to thee, never more will I come.

LXVI
(121)

"Ἄνθε' ἀμέργοισαν παῖδ' ἄγαν ἀπαλάν.

A maiden most tender, gathering flowers.

LXVII
(122)

Πόλυ πάκτιδος ἀδυμελεστέρα, χρύσω χρυσοτέρα.

Far sweeter-sounding than the harp, more gold than gold.

LXVIII
(129)

Ῥοδοπήχεις καὶ ἑλικώπιδες καὶ καλλιπύργοι καὶ μελίφωνοι.

Maidens with rosy arms, and glancing eyes, fair cheeks, and voice of honey.

LXIX
(133)

Hesperus

Ἀστέρων πάντων ὁ κάλιστος.

Of all stars the fairest.

LXX
(136)

Ἀλλ' οὐ γὰρ θέμις ἐν μοισοπόλῳ οἰκίᾳ
θρῆνον ἔμμεναι· οὐκ ἄμμι πρέπει τάδε.

But it is not right that there be mourning in the house of a poet; these things befit us not.

LXXI

(137)

Τὸ θνάσκειν κακόν· οὕτω κεκρίκασι θεοί·
ἔθνασκον γὰρ ἂν εἴπερ κάλον ἦν τόδε.

Death is evil, the gods have so judged; for if it were good, they would have died.

ALCAEUS

Alcaeus was an aristocrat of Mitylene in Lesbos, and belongs to the close of the seventh and the earlier part of the sixth century B.C. He was engaged in constant political strife with men such as Myrsilus (referred to in Frag. viii.), who endeavoured to establish themselves as tyrants of Mitylene. Part of his turbulent life was spent in exile and foreign warfare. The distractions of the state led ultimately to the appointment of Pittacus as dictator (Frag. xviii.), who exercised a just and wise rule. During his government Alcaeus and his brother nobles attempted to reinstate themselves by arms, but were defeated. Alcaeus was taken prisoner, but received his liberty from Pittacus.

(5)

To Hermes

Χαῖρε Κυλλάνας ὃ μέδεις, σὲ γάρ μοι
θῦμος ὕμνην, τὸν κορύφαις ἐν αὔταις
Μαῖα γέννατο Κρονίδᾳ μίγεισα.

Hail, thou that art Lord of Cyllene, for thee it is my desire to sing, whom Maia, wedding the son of Chronos, bore on the very mountain tops.

II

(9)

To Athene

Ὤνασσ' Ἀθανάα πολεμαδόκος,
ἅ ποι Κορωνήας ἐπὶ πίσεων
ναύω πάροιθεν ἀμφι(βαίνεις)
Κωραλίω ποτάμω παρ' ὄχθαις.

Queen Athene, steadfast in battle, that on the meadows of Coronea keepest ward before thy temple, by the banks of the river Coralius.

III
(13 B)

Love

Δεινότατον θέων,
(τὸν) γέννατ' εὐπέδιλλος Ἶρις
χρυσοκόμᾳ Ζεφύρῳ μίγεισα.

Most terrible of the gods, whom fair-sandalled Iris bore to the golden-haired Zephyr.

IV
(15)

Μαρμαίρει δὲ μέγας δόμος χάλκῳ· πᾶσα δ' Ἄρη
κεκόσμηται στέγα
λάμπραισιν κυνίαισι, καττᾶν λεῦκοι κατύπερθεν
ἵππιοι λόφοι
νεύοισιν, κεφάλαισιν ἄνδρων ἀγάλματα· χάλκιαι
δὲ πασσάλοις
κρύπτοισιν περικείμεναι λάμπραι κνάμιδες, ἄρκος
ἰσχύρω βέλευς,
θώρακές τε νέοι λίνω κοΐλαί τε κατ' ἄσπιδες
βεβλήμεναι·
παρ δὲ Χαλκίδικαι σπάθαι, παρ δὲ ζώματα πόλλα
καὶ κυπάττιδες·
τῶν οὐκ ἔστι λάθεσθ', ἐπειδὴ πρώτιστ' ὑπὸ Ϝέργον
ἔσταμεν τόδε.

The great house flashes with bronze, and the whole dwelling is decked in honour of Ares with shining helmets, over which white horsehair

ests, ornaments of the heads of warriors, nod
om above. And gleaming brazen greaves,
arding off the fierce dart, cover the pegs on
hich they hang, and there are new linen corse-
ts and hollow shields laid upon the ground.
nd by them are swords from Chalcis, and many
 apron-piece and jerkin. These it is not meet
at we forget, so soon as we set ourselves to this
onflict.

v
(16)

. . . βλήχρων ἀνέμων ἀχείμαντοι πνόαι.

The unvexed breath of faint breezes.

vi
(18)

The Ship of the State

Ἀσυνέτημι τῶν ἀνέμων στάσιν·
τὸ μὲν γὰρ ἔνθεν κῦμα κυλίνδεται,
 τὸ δ' ἔνθεν· ἄμμες δ' ἂν τὸ μέσσον
 νᾶϊ φορήμεθα σὺν μελαίνᾳ,
χείμωνι μοχθεῦντες μεγάλῳ μάλα·
περ μὲν γὰρ ἄντλος ἰστοπέδαν ἔχει,
 λαῖφος δὲ πᾶν ζάδηλον ἤδη
 καὶ λάκιδες μέγαλαι κατ' αὖτο·
χόλαισι δ' ἄγκοιναι.

I understand not the strife of the winds, for
ow the wave is rolled from this side, and now

from that, and we are carried in the midst in our dark ship, labouring sore in the great storm. For water surrounds the mast-step, and the whole sail can now be seen through, and there are great rents in it, and the yard-ropes are loosened.

VII
(19)

Τὸ δηὖτε κῦμα τῶν προτέρων ὄνω
στείχει, παρέξει δ' ἄμμι πόνον πόλυν
ἄντλην, ἐπεί κε νᾶος ἐμβᾷ
νή (ατα).

Again comes the wave higher than those before, and will make us prove the fulness of much woe, when it strikes the ship's hold.

VIII
(20)

Νῦν χρὴ μεθύσθην καί τινα πρὸς βίαν
πώνην, ἐπειδὴ κάτθανε Μύρσιλος.

Now must one be drunk and carouse riotously, since Myrsilus is dead.

IX
(23)

Ἄνδρες πόληος πύργος ἀρεύιοι.

Men of valour are a city's bulwark.

X

(25)

Ὤνηρ οὗτος ὁ μαιόμενος τὸ μέγα κρέτος
ἀντρέψει τάχα τὰν πόλιν· ἁ δ' ἔχεται ῥόπας.

This man, seeking after supreme dominion, will quickly overthrow the city: it hangs upon a turn of the scale.

XI

(26)

Οὐδέ πω Ποσείδαν
ἄλμυρον ἐστυφέλιξε πόντον·
οἶον (πέδον) γᾶς γὰρ πέλεται σέων.

Not yet has Poseidon smitten the salt sea, for it is smooth as the floor of the gods' earth.

XII

(27)

Ἔπταζον ὥστ' ὄρνιθες ὦκυν
αἴετον ἐξαπίνας φάνευτα.

They shrank like birds from a swift eagle, when suddenly he appears.

XIII

(30)

Τὸ γὰρ
Ἄρευϊ κατθάνην κάλον.

For it is glorious to die in service to Ares.

XIV
(33)

To His Brother Antimenidas

ἦλθες ἐκ περάτων γᾶς ἐλεφαντίναν
λάβαν τῶ ξίφεος χρυσοδέταν ἔχων,
(ἐπειδὴ μέγαν ἆθλον Βαβυλωνίοις
συμμάχεις τέλεσας, ῥύσαό τ' ἐκ πόνων),
κτέννais ἄνδρα μαχαίταν βασιληΐων
παλαίσταν ἀπολείποντα μόνον μίαν
παχέων ἀπὺ πέμπων.

Thou hast come from the ends of the earth, bearing a sword with gold-bound ivory hilt, for thou didst bring to a close for the men of Babylon a great contest, making thyself their ally, and didst free them from toils, slaying a man that was a warrior, who lacked but one hand's breadth of five royal cubits.

XV
(34)

Ὕει μὲν ὀ Ζεύς, ἐκ δ' ὀράνω μέγας
χείμων, πεπάγασιν δ' ὑδάτων ῥόαι.
*   *   *   *
*   *   *   *

κάββαλε τὸν χείμων', ἐπὶ μὲν τίθεις
πῦρ, ἐν δὲ κίρναις οἶνον ἀφειδέως
μέλιχρον, αὐτὰρ ἀμφὶ κόρσᾳ
μάλθακον ἀμφιτίθη[1] γνόφαλλον.

Zeus rains, and there comes a great storm from

---
[1] Bergk, ἀμφι . . . γνόφαλλον.

'the sky, and the streams of water are frozen . . . Fight the cold down, piling up the fire, and mixing without stint the honey-sweet wine, and place a soft cushion about thy head.

XVI
(35)

Οὐ χρὴ κάκοισι θῦμον ἐπιτρέπην·
προκόψομεν γὰρ οὐδὲν ἀσάμενοι,
ὦ Βύκχι, φάρμακον δ' ἄριστον
οἶνον ἐνεικαμένοις μεθύσθην.

It is not well to turn the mind to troubles, for we shall profit nothing, O Bacchus, by grieving; but the best remedy is that we have wine brought and make us drunk.

XVII
(36)

Ἀλλ' ἀνήτω μὲν περὶ ταῖς δέραισιν
περθέτω πλέκταις ὑποθύμιδάς τις.
καδ δὲ χευάτω μύρον ἆδυ κατ τῶ
στήθεος ἄμμι.

But let some one place about our necks wreathed garlands of dill, and pour fragrant myrrh down upon our breast.

XVIII
(37)

Τὸν κακοπάτριδα
Πιττακον πόλιος τᾶς διχόλω καὶ βαρυδαίμονος
ἐστάσαντο τύραννον μέγ᾽ ἐπαινέοντες ἀόλλεες.

They all with great acclaim made low-born Pittacus tyrant of the hapless city, divided against itself.

XIX
(39)

Τέγγε πνεύμονας οἴνῳ· τὸ γὰρ ἄστρον περιτέλλεται,
ἁ δ᾽ ὤρα χαλέπα, πάντα δὲ δίψαισ᾽ ὑπὸ καύματος.
ἄχει δ᾽ ἐκ πετάλων Fάδεα τέττιξ, πτερύγων δ᾽ ὕπο
κακχέει λιγύραν (πύκνον) ἀοίδαν, (θέρος) ὅπποτα
φλόγιον κατὰ γᾶν πεπτάμενον πάντα καταυάνῃ.
ἄνθει καὶ σκόλυμος· νῦν δὲ γύναικες μιαρώταται,
λέπτοι δ᾽ ἄνδρες, ἐπεὶ καὶ κεφάλαν καὶ γόνα Σείριος
ἄζει.

Wet the throat with wine, for the dog-star rises, and the season weighs heavy, and all things are athirst with heat. And the cicada sounds sweetly from among the leaves, and pours shrill notes from its wings unceasingly, while fiery summer, spread over the earth, dries all things up. In flower, too, is the golden thistle; and now women are fullest of desire, but men are languid, for Sirius scorches head and knee.

XX
(41)

Πίνωμεν· τί τὸ λύχνον μένομεν; δάκτυλος ἀμέρα.
καδ δ' ἄειρε κυλίχναις μεγάλαις, αἴτ' ὅτι Οἴκι λαῖς·
οἶνον γὰρ Σεμέλας καὶ Δίος υἶος λαθικάδεα
ἀνθρώποισιν ἔδωκ'· ἔγχεε κίρναις ἕνα καὶ δύο
πλέαις κακ κεφάλας, ἁ δ' ἀτέρα τὰν ἀτέραν κύλιξ
ὠθήτω.

Let us drink; why wait we for the lamp? There remains but a finger's breadth of day. Lift down the great cups, or whatever thou wilt, Oecis, for the son of Semele and Zeus gave to men wine that banishes care. Fill them full above the brim, mixing one measure of water and two of wine, and let goblet follow quick upon goblet.

XXI
(42)
Alcaeus Grown Old

Κατ τᾶς πόλλα παθοίσας κεφάλας κακχεάτω μύρον
καὶ κατ τῶ πολίω στήθεος.

Let some one pour myrrh over the toil-worn head and hoary breast.

XXII
(44)

Μηδὲν ἄλλο φυτεύσῃς πρότερον δένδριον ἀμπέλω.

Plant no other tree before the vine.

XXIII
(45)

Ἦρος ἀνθεμόεντος ἐπάϊον ἐρχομένοιο.

I heard the flower-decked spring approaching.

XXIV
(46)

Κέλομαί τινα τὸν χαρίεντα Μένωνα κάλεσσαι,
αἰ χρὴ συμποσίας ἐπ' ὄνασιν ἔμοι γεγένησθαι.

I bid them call the fair Menon, if I am to have joy of the revel.

XXV
(47)

Ἄλλοτα μὲν μελιάδεος, ἄλλοτα δ'
ὀξυτέρω τριβόλων ἀρυτήμενοι.

Drawing wine sometimes honey-sweet, and sometimes more sharp than a prickly burr.

XXVI
(49)

Ὥς γὰρ δήποτ' Ἀριστόδαμόν φαισ' οὐκ ἀπάλαμνον
ἐν Σπάρτᾳ λόγον
εἴπην· χρήματ' ἄνηρ, πένιχρος δ' οὐδεὶς πέλετ' ἔσλος
οὐδὲ τίμιος.

For thus they say Aristodemus once spake in Sparta no foolish word: wealth makes the man, and no one that is poor is good or honoured.

XXVII
(50)

Δοκίμοι δ' ἄριστος ἔμμεναι
πώνων· αἰ δέ κ' ὀνῆσι Ϝᾶδυς περὶ φρένας οἶνος, αὖ
  δὶς ἄθλιος.
κᾶπος γὰρ κεφάλαν κατίσχει· τὸν Ϝὸν θαμὰ θῦμον
  αἰτιάμενος
πεδαμενόμενός τ' ἀσάζει· τόκ' οὐκέτι Ϝανδάνει· πῶ
  τάνδε, πῶ.

And he seems when drinking to be most blest. But if the sweet wine gives him joy at heart, afterwards he is twice accurst. For heaviness weighs down his head, and, chiding often his own soul and repenting, he is possessed with grief. Then no longer does the strain 'Drink, drink this cup,' please him.

XXVIII
(53)

Οἶνος γὰρ ἀνθρώποις δίοπτρον.

For wine is a spying-glass upon men.

XXIX
(55)

Written, by way of compliment, in Sappho's characteristic metre. Cf. Sappho, Frag. xvii.

Ἰόπλοκ' ἄγνα μελλιχόμειδε Σάπφοι,
θέλω τι Ϝείπην, ἀλλά με κωλύει αἴδως.

Violet-weaving, pure, soft-smiling Sappho, something I wish to say, but shame prevents me.

XXX
(56)

Δέξαι με κωμάζοντα, δέξαι, λίσσομαί σε, λίσσομαι.

Receive me, who come with revel, receive, I entreat, I entreat thee.

XXXI
(57)

Οἶνος, ὦ φίλε παῖ, καὶ ἀλάθεα.

Wine and truth, dear child.

XXXII
(62)

Κόλπῳ σ' ἐδέξαντ' ἄγναι Χάριτες, Κρίνοι.

The maiden Graces received thee, Crino, in their bosom.

XXXIII
(63)

Ἄεισον ἄμμι τὰν ἰόκολπον.

Sing to us her of the dusky breast.

XXXIV
(76)

Καί κ' οὐδὲν ἐκ δένος γένοιτο.

And from nothing nothing would come.

XXXV
(82)

Νῦν δ' (αὖτ') οὖτος ἐπικρέτει
κινήσαις τὸν ἀπ' ἴρας πύματον λίθον.

But now again this one prevails, moving his last piece forward from the line.

XXXVI
(83)

Αἴκ' εἴπῃς, τὰ θέλεις, (αὖτος) ἀκούσαις κε, τά κ' οὐ θέλοις.

If you say the things that you wish, you will yourself hear the things that you would not wish.

XXXVII
(84)

Ὄρνιθες τίνες οἴδ'; ὠκεάνω γᾶς τ' ἀπὺ περράτων
ἦλθον πανέλοπες ποικιλόδειροι τανυσίπτεροι.

What birds are these? From the ends of the sea and earth they have come, broad-winged mallards with necks of many-coloured plumage.

XXXVIII
(92)

Ἀργάλεον πενία κάκον ἄσχετον, ἃ μέγα δάμναις
λᾶον ἀμαχανίᾳ σὺν ἀδελφέᾳ.

A grievous, resistless ill art thou, O Poverty, that with thy sister Helplessness dost heavily oppress the people.

VERSES ATTRIBUTED TO THE SAGES

The following names, Pittacus, Bias, Chilo, and Thales are those of four of the seven Wise Men of Greece, who belong to the early part of the sixth century. Pittacus has been already mentioned in connection with Alcaeus as the ruler of Mitylene. Bias was a native of Priene in Ionia, and was living as late as the subjugation of the Ionian cities by the Persians. Chilo belonged to Sparta, where he held the post of ephor. Thales of Miletus is the first recorded figure in Greek philosophy.

PITTACUS

Ἔχοντα δεῖ τόξον τε καὶ ἰοδόκον φαρέτραν
στείχειν ποτὶ φῶτα κακόν·
πιστὸν γὰρ οὐδὲν γλῶσσα διὰ στόματος
λαλεῖ διχόμυθον ἔχουσι καρδίᾳ νόημα.

With bow and arrow-holding quiver must one draw near to an evil man; for the tongue utters nothing trustworthy through the lips of those who have in their heart a double-speaking thought.

BIAS

Ἀστοῖσιν ἀρέσκεο πᾶσιν ἐν πόλει, ᾗκε μένῃς·
πλείσταν γὰρ ἔχει χάριν· αὐθάδης δὲ τρόπος
πολλάκι δὴ βλαβερὰν ἐξέλαμψεν ἄταν.

Make thyself pleasing to all the townsfolk in the city, wheresoever thou dost abide, for that brings most favour; but from a stubborn spirit mischievous ruin has often flamed forth.

CHILO

Ἐν μὲν λιθίναις ἀκόναις ὁ χρυσὸς ἐξετάζεται
διδοὺς βάσανον φανεράν·
ἐν δὲ χρυσῷ
ἀνδρῶν ἀγαθῶν τε κακῶν τε νοῦς ἔδωκ᾽ ἔλεγχον.

Gold yields a clear test of itself when tried upon the touchstone, and the mind of good men and bad yields proof of itself in gold.

THALES

Οὔτι τὰ πολλὰ ἔπη φρονίμην ἀπεφήνατο δόξαν·
ἕν τι μάτευε σοφόν,
ἕν τι κεδνὸν αἱροῦ·
παύσεις γὰρ ἀνδρῶν κωτίλων γλώσσας ἀπεραντο-
    λόγους.

It is not many words that are a sign of prudent thought. Seek one wise thing, choose one trustworthy thing, for so thou wilt make to cease the endlessly prating tongues of chatterers.

STESICHORUS

Stesichorus (*circ.* 630-550 B.C.) was a native of Himera in Sicily. The most important part of his work consisted in the reproduction of the old epic stories in lyric form.

The first three fragments are from the Geryoneis, the account of the expedition of Hercules to seize the cattle of Geryon in the island of Gades. The first fragment describes the birthplace of Eurythion, Geryon's herdsman, Erythea being an old name for Gades, and Tartessus for the river Baetis. The second refers to the entertainment given to Hercules, after his return from the expedition, by the centaur Pholus. The third speaks of the cup in which Helios performed his nightly voyage across the ocean from west to east. It was in this cup, lent by Helios, that Hercules had reached Gades.

I

(5)

Ταρτησσοῦ ποταμοῦ σχεδὸν ἀντιπέρας κλεινᾶς
  Ἐρυθείας
ἐν κευθμῶνι πέτρας παρὰ παγὰς ἀπείρονας ἀργυρο-
  ρίζους.

Near the river Tartessus, over against famed Erythea, in a hollow of the rock by the never-failing, deep-rooted fount of silver ore.

II

(7)

Σκύπφειον δὲ λαβὼν δέπας ἔμμετρον ὡς τριλάγυνον
πῖνεν ἐπισχόμενος, τό ῥά οἱ παρέθηκε Φόλος κεράσας.

And taking a bowl-shaped cup, holding three flagons, which Pholus mixed and set before him, he put it to his lips and drank.

III
(8)

Ἀέλιος δ' Ὑπεριονίδας δέπας ἐσκατέβαινεν
χρύσεον, ὄφρα δι' Ὠκεανοῖο περάσας
ἀφίκοιθ' ἱερᾶς ποτὶ βένθεα νυκτὸς ἐρεμνᾶς
ποτὶ ματέρα κουριδίαν τ' ἄλοχον παῖδάς τε φίλους·
ὁ δ' ἐς ἄλσος ἔβα
δάφναισι κατάσκιον ποσσὶ πάϊς Διός.

And Helios, son of Hyperion, went down into the golden cup, that crossing the ocean he might come to the depths of dark, holy night, to his mother and wedded wife and loved children. But the son of Zeus turned his steps to a laurel-shaded grove.

IV
(26)

From the poem attacking Helen, in consequence of which Stesichorus was reported to have been struck with blindness.

Οὕνεκα Τυνδάρεος
ῥέζων ποτὲ πᾶσι θεοῖς μούνας λάθετ' ἠπιοδώρω
Κύπριδος· κείνα δὲ Τυνδαρέου κόραις
χολωσαμένη διγάμους τε καὶ τριγάμους τίθησιν
καὶ λιπεσάνορας.

Because Tyndareus once, when sacrificing to all the gods, forgot bountiful Cypris alone. And she, being angered with the daughters of Tyndarcus, made them to be twice and thrice married, and to forsake their lords.

V

(29)

The Wedding of Helen and Menelaus

Πολλὰ μὲν Κυδώνια μᾶλα ποτέρριπτον ποτὶ δίφρον
    ἄνακτι,
πολλὰ δὲ μύρσινα φύλλα
καὶ ῥοδίνους στεφάνους ἴων τε κορωνίδας οὔλας.

Many apples of Cydon they cast at the king's chariot, and many leaves of myrtle, and garlands of roses, and twined wreaths of violets.

VI

(32)

From the Palinode, or recantation, addressed to Helen, after writing which the poet's sight was restored. In it he declared that it was only a phantom Helen that had accompanied Paris.

Οὐκ ἔστ' ἔτυμος λόγος οὗτος·
οὐδ' ἔβας ἐν ναυσὶν εὐσέλμοις
οὐδ' ἵκεο πέργαμα Τροίας.

This tale is not true. Thou didst not go in the decked ships, nor didst thou come to the towers of Troy.

VII

(35)

Μοῦσα, σὺ μὲν . . . μετ' ἐμοῦ
κλείουσα θεῶν τε γάμους ἀνδρῶν τε δαῖτας καὶ
θαλίας μακάρων.

Thou, O Muse, celebrating with me the marriages of the gods, and the banquetings of men, and the festivals of the immortals.

VIII

(37)

Τοιάδε χρὴ Χαρίτων δαμώματα καλλικόμων
ὑμνεῖν Φρύγιον μέλος ἐξευρόντας ἁβρῶς ἦρος ἐπερχομένου.

Such songs of the fair-haired Graces must they chant for the people's hearing, fashioning delicately a Phrygian strain, when spring comes in.

IX

(42)

Clytemnestra's vision of Agamemnon or Orestes

Τᾷ δὲ δράκων ἐδόκησεν μολεῖν κάρα βεβροτωμένος
ἄκρον·
ἐκ δ' ἄρα τοῦ βασιλεὺς Πλεισθενίδας ἐφάνη.

And it seemed to her that a dragon came with the stain of blood upon its topmost crest; and after that there appeared the king, the son of Pleisthenes.

X
(44)

Introduction to the Rhadina, so named from its heroine Rhadina of Samos.

Ἄγε Μοῦσα λίγει', ἄρξον ἀοιδᾶς ἐρατωνύμου
Σαμίων περὶ παίδων ἐρατᾷ φθεγγομένα λύρᾳ.

Come, Muse of the clear note, begin a sweet-named strain telling of the children of Samos, lifting up thy voice with the lovely lyre.

XI
(49)

Κοιλωνύχων ἵππων πρύτανις, Ποσειδάν.

Poseidon, lord of hollow-hoofed horses.

XII
(50)

Μάλα τοι μελιστᾶν
παιγμοσύνας τε φιλεῖ μολπάς τ' Ἀπόλλων·
κάδεα δὲ στοναχάς τ' Ἀΐδας ἔλαχεν.

Dearly Apollo loves the mirth and songs of minstrels, but cares and wailing are the portion of Hades.

XIII

(51)

'Ατελέστατα γὰρ καὶ ἀμάχανα τοὺς θανόντας κλαίειν.

For no least issue or help is there in mourning the dead.

XIV

(52)

Θανόντος ἀνδρὸς πᾶσ' ἀπόλλυται ποτ' ἀνθρώπων χάρις.

When a man has died, all the regard of mortals for him sooner or later perishes.

IBYCUS

This poet, who belongs in date to the second half of the sixth century B.C., was a native of Rhegium in the extreme south of Italy. He lived at the court of Polycrates, tyrant of Samos, who was an enlightened patron of literature. He partly followed Stesichorus in treating of mythological stories, but his most characteristic remains are impassioned love-poems of a highly personal kind. As such, these latter are unique in being intended, as is shown by the metre, to be sung not by a single performer, but chorally.

I

(1)

Ἦρι μὲν αἵ τε Κυδώνιαι
μηλίδες ἀρδόμεναι ῥοᾶν
ἐκ ποταμῶν, ἵνα παρθένων
κῆπος ἀκήρατος, αἵ τ' οἰνανθίδες
αὐξόμεναι σκιεροῖσιν ὑφ' ἔρνεσιν
οἰναρέοις θαλέθοισιν· ἐμοὶ δ' ἔρος
οὐδεμίαν κατάκοιτος ὥραν, ἅθ' ὑπὸ στεροπᾶς φλέγων
Θρηΐκιος βορέας,
ἄσσων παρὰ Κύπριδος ἀζαλέαις μανίαισιν ἐρεμνὸς
   ἀθαμβής
ἐγκρατέως παιδόθεν φυλάσσει
ἡμετέρας φρένας.

There, where lies the garden unprofaned of the maiden nymphs, Cydonian apple-trees, watered with streams from the rivers, and vine-buds, swelling beneath the shadowing tendrils, put forth their leaves in spring. But love, knowing for me no time of rest, like Thracian Boreas raging amid the lightning-flashes, speeds dark and unrelenting from the Cyprian goddess, and from boyhood tyrannously besets my heart with parching frenzy.

II
(2)

Ἔρος αὖτέ με κυανέοισιν ὑπὸ βλεφάροις τακέρ'
 ὄμμασι δερκόμενος
κηλήμασι παντοδαποῖς ἐς ἄπειρα
δίκτυα Κύπριδός με βάλλει·
ἦ μὰν τρομέω νιν ἐπερχόμενον,
ὥστε φερέζυγος ἵππος ἀεθλοφόρος ποτὶ γήραϊ
 ἀέκων
σὺν ὄχεσφι θοοῖς ἐς ἅμιλλαν ἔβα.

Again does love, looking upon me with melting glance beneath his dark eyelids, drive me by manifold enchantments into the endless snares of Aphrodite. Verily, I tremble at his approach, even as the yoke-bearing horse, the winner of prizes, when he is nigh to old age, goes unwillingly with the swift chariot into the contest.

III
(3)

Φλεγέθων, ᾇπερ διὰ νύκτα μακρὰν σείρια παμφανόωντα.

Glowing like stars shining bright through the long night.

IV

(5)

Εὐρύαλε, γλαυκέων Χαρίτων θάλος,

*   *   *   *

καλλικόμων μελέδημα, σὲ μὲν Κύπρις
ἅ τ' ἀγανοβλέφαρος Πειθὼ ῥοδέοισιν ἐν ἄνθεσι
θρέψαν.

Euryalus, nursling of the bright-eyed Graces, joy of the fair-tressed loves, the Cyprian goddess and gentle-eyed Persuasion reared thee among the blossoms of the rose.

V

(6)

Μύρτα τε καὶ ἴα καὶ ἑλίχρυσος,
μᾶλά τε καὶ ῥόδα καὶ τέρεινα δάφνα.

Myrtle-berries and violets and marigold, apples and roses and tender laurel.

VI

(7)

Τᾶμος ἄϋπνος κλυτὸς ὄρθρος ἐγείρησιν ἀηδόνας.

Then the unsleeping, glorious dawn awakes the nightingales.

VII

(9)

Γλαυκώπιδα Κασσάνδραν
ἐρασιπλόκαμον κούραν Πριάμου φᾶμις ἔχῃσι βροτῶν.

The voice of men tells of bright-eyed Cassandra, fair-haired daughter of Priam.

VIII

(16)

Hercules and the Molionidae

Τούς τε λευκίππους κόρους
τέκνα Μολιόνας κτάνον,
ἅλικας ἰσοπάλους, ἐνιγυίους,
ἀμφοτέρους γεγαῶτας ἐν ὠέῳ
ἀργυρέῳ . . .

And I slew the youths with white steeds, the sons of Molione, equal in age and equally matched, joined in one body, twin-born in an egg of silver sheen.

IX

(21)

Δαρὸν δ' ἄνεω χρόνον ἧστο τάφει πεπαγώς.

And for a long time he sat silent, keeping close to the tomb.

X
(22)

The reference is to the island of Ortygia having been joined by a mole to Syracuse.

Παρὰ χέρσον
λίθινον ἔκλεκτον παλάμαισι βροτῶν·
πρόσθε δέ νιν πεδ' ἀναριτᾶν
ἰχθύες ὠμοφάγοι νέμοντο.

Along a causeway of stones brought together by men's hands; but before ravening fish and sea-mussels inhabited there.

XI
(24)

Δέδοικα, μή τι παρ θεοῖς
ἀμβλακὼν τιμὰν πρὸς ἀνθρώπων ἀμείψω.

I fear lest, sinning in the sight of the gods, I win in exchange honour from men.

XII
(26)

(Τάχα κέν τις ἀνὴρ) Ἔριδος ποτὶ μάργον ἔχων στόμα
ἀντία δῆριν ἐμοὶ κορύσσοι.

Some one, perchance, moving forward the raging lips of strife, will prepare battle against me.

XIII
(27)

Οὐκ ἔστιν ἀποφθιμένοις ζωᾶς ἔτι φάρμακον εὑρεῖν.

There is no finding again for the dead a remedy to bring back life.

XIV
(28)

Ποτᾶται δ' ἐν ἀλλοτρίῳ χάει.

And flies in unknown wastes of air.

ANACREON

Anacreon was a native of Teos, an Ionian city on the coast of Asia Minor, and his activity extends from about 530 B.C. to early in the next century. He lived under the protection of Polycrates, and after his death under that of Hipparchus at Athens, where he must have been contemporary with Simonides. His position as a court-poet naturally led to the absence from his work of political and serious interests, and he comes before us as a typical representative of the pleasure-loving Ionian temperament.

1

(1)

The goddess is invoked in connection with one of her seats of worship, Leucophris, a city of Magnesia, on the Lethaeus.

Γουνοῦμαί σ', ἐλαφηβόλε,
ξανθὴ παῖ Διός, ἀγρίων
   δέσποιν' Ἄρτεμι θηρῶν·
ἣ κου νῦν ἐπὶ Ληθαίου
δίνῃσι θρασυκαρδίων
ἀνδρῶν ἐσκατορᾷς πόλιν
χαίρουσ'· οὐ γὰρ ἀνημέρους
ποιμαίνεις πολιήτας.

Thee, Artemis, I entreat, huntress of stags, golden-haired daughter of Zeus, mistress of savage beasts, who now somewhere by the eddies of Lethaeus lookest down with joy upon a city of brave-hearted men;—for thou shepherdest no ungentle citizens.

II

(2)

To Dionysus

Ὦναξ, ᾧ δαμάλης Ἔρως
καὶ Νύμφαι κυανώπιδες
πορφυρέη τ' Ἀφροδίτη
συμπαίζουσιν· ἐπιστρέφεαι δ'
ὑψηλῶν κορυφὰς ὀρέων,
γουνοῦμαί σε· σὺ δ' εὐμενής
ἔλθ' ἡμῖν, κεχαρισμένης δ'
εὐχωλῆς ἐπακούειν.
Κλευβούλῳ δ' ἀγαθὸς γενεῦ
σύμβουλος· τὸν ἐμὸν δ' ἔρωτ',
ὦ Δεύνυσε, δέχεσθαι.

King, with whom Love the conqueror, and the dark-eyed Nymphs, and radiant Aphrodite sport, who rangest over the tops of the lofty mountains, thee I entreat. And do thou come graciously disposed to us, and hearken to my prayer, giving thy favour. Be to Cleobulus a good counsellor, and bid him receive, O Dionysus, my love.

III

(3)

Κλευβούλου μὲν ἔγωγ' ἐρῶ,
Κλευβούλῳ δ' ἐπιμαίνομαι,
Κλεύβουλον δὲ διοσκέω.

Cleobulus I love, and for Cleobulus I am distraught, and upon Cleobulus I fix steadfastly my eyes.

IV

(4)

Ὦ παῖ παρθένιον βλέπων,
δίζημαί σε, σὺ δ' οὐ κοεῖς,
οὐκ εἰδώς, ὅτι τῆς ἐμῆς
ψυχῆς ἡνιοχεύεις.

Boy with a maiden's eyes, I seek after thee; but thou heedest not, unwitting that thou holdest the reins of my heart.

V

(6)

Μεὶς μὲν δὴ Ποσιδηϊών
ἕστηκεν, νεφέλας δ' ὕδωρ
βαρύνει, Δία τ' ἄγριοι
χειμῶνες κατάγουσιν.

It is the month of Poseidon, and water makes heavy the clouds, and fierce storms bring down Zeus from the sky.

VI

(7)

Σὺ γὰρ ἦς ἔμοιγ'
ἀστεμφής.

For thou wast unrelenting to me.

VII
(8)

Ἐγὼ δ' οὔτ' ἂν Ἀμαλθίης
βουλοίμην κέρας, οὔτ' ἔτεα
πεντήκοντά τε καὶ ἑκατόν
Ταρτησσοῦ βασιλεῦσαι.

But for me, I would not wish for the horn of Amalthea, nor to be for a hundred and fifty years the lord of Tartessus.

VIII
(13 A)

Ἔρως παρθένιος πόθῳ
στίλβων καὶ γεγανωμένος.

Love for a maiden, love radiant and glad with desire.

IX
(14)

Σφαίρῃ δηὖτέ με πορφυρέῃ
βάλλων χρυσοκόμης Ἔρως
νήνι ποικιλοσαμβάλῳ
  συμπαίζειν προκαλεῖται·
ἡ δ', ἐστὶν γὰρ ἀπ' εὐκτίτου
Λέσβου, τὴν μὲν ἐμὴν κόμην,
λευκὴ γάρ, καταμέμφεται,
  πρὸς δ' ἄλλον τινὰ χάσκει.

Golden-haired love, casting at me again his purple ball, challenges me to sport with a maid with broidered sandals.   But she, for she is from fair-built Lesbos, slights my hairs, since they are white, and gazes love-lost upon another.

X

(15)

Οὐ δηὖτ' ἔμπεδός εἰμι,
οὐδ' ἀστοῖσι προσηνής.

I am not of constant mind, nor gracious to the townsfolk.

XI

(17)

Ἠρίστησα μὲν ἰτρίου λεπτοῦ μικρὸν ἀποκλάς,
οἴνου δ' ἐξέπιον κάδον, νῦν δ' ἁβρῶς ἐρόεσσαν
ψάλλω πηκτίδα τῇ φίλῃ κωμάζων παιδὶ ἁβρῇ.

For the mid-day meal I broke off a small piece of light wheaten cake, and drained a jar of wine; and now daintily I strike the sweet harp, making song to a loved and dainty maid.

XII

(18)

Ψάλλω δ' εἴκοσι (Λυδόν)
χορδῇσιν μαγάδην ἔχων, ὦ Λεύκαστι, σὺ δ' ἡβᾷς.

I play, Leucaspis, on a Lydian harp of twenty strings,—and thou art in the fairness of thy youth.

XIII

(19)

Ἀρθεὶς δηὖτ' ἀπὸ Λευκάδος
πέτρης ἐς πολιὸν κῦμα κολυμβῶ μεθύων ἔρωτι.

Springing again from the Leucadian rock, I plunge, drunk with love, into the grey sea.

XIV

(20)

Τίς ἐρασμίην
τρέψας θυμὸν ἐς ἥβην τερένων ἡμιόπων ὑπ' αὐλῶν
ὀρχεῖται;

Who, turning his soul to sweet mirth, dances to the sound of soft flutes with but three stops?

XV

(21)

An attack upon Artemon, his successful rival in the affections of Eurypyle.

Ξανθῇ δέ γ' Εὐρυπύλῃ μέλει
ὁ περιφόρητος Ἄρτεμων·
πρὶν μὲν ἔχων βερβέριον, καλύμματ' ἐσφηκωμένα,
καὶ ξυλίνους ἀστραγάλους ἐν ὡσί, καὶ ψιλὸν περί
 πλευρῇσι (δέρμ' ἥει) βοός,
νήπλυτον εἴλυμα κακῆς ἀσπίδος, ἀρτοπώλισιν

κἀθελοπόρνοισιν ὁμιλέων ὁ πονηρὸς Ἀρτέμων,
    κίβδηλον εὑρίσκων βίον·
πολλὰ μὲν ἐν δουρὶ δεθεὶς αὐχένα, πολλὰ δ' ἐν τροχῷ,
πολλὰ δὲ νῶτον σκυτίνῃ μάστιγι θωμιχθείς, κόμην
    πώγωνά τ' ἐκτετιλμένος.
νῦν δ' ἐπιβαίνει σατινέων, χρύσεα φορέων καθέρματα
πάϊς Κύκης, καὶ σκιαδίσκην ἐλεφαντίνην φορεῖ
    γυναιξὶν αὔτως.

But to golden-haired Eurypyle Artemon of evil fame is dear. Once he went wearing the pointed head-gear of a turban, with wooden earrings in his ears, and a worn ox-skin, the unwashed covering of a sorry shield, round his sides, consorting with baking-women and the vilest strumpets, Artemon the base, winning a trickster's livelihood; his neck often bound in the stocks and to the wheel, his back often lashed with a leathern scourge, his hair and beard plucked out. But now he mounts upon a car, he, Cyce's son, decked with golden earrings, and carries like a woman a sunshade of ivory.

XVI

(24)

Ἀναπέτομαι δὴ πρὸς Ὄλυμπον πτερύγεσσι κούφαις
διὰ τὸν Ἔρωτ'· οὐ γὰρ ἐμοὶ παῖς ἐθέλει συνηβᾶν.

Up to Olympus I fly on light wings because of Love, for there is a boy who consents not to take dalliance with me.

XVII

(25)

("Ερως), ὥς μ' ἐσιδὼν γένειον
ὑποπόλιον χρυσοφαέννων πτερύγων ἀήταις
παραπέτεται.

When Love, seeing me with grey-sprinkled beard, flies by with a windy sweep of his gold-bright pinions.

XVIII

(28)

Ἀσπίδα ῥίψας ποταμοῦ καλλιρόου παρ' ὄχθας.

Casting away my shield by the banks of the fair-flowing river.

XIX

(32)

Ὠινοχόει δ' ἀμφίπολος μελιχρὸν
οἶνον, τρικύαθον κελέβην ἔχουσα.

And a handmaiden was pouring the sweet wine, having a beaker that held three cupfuls.

XX

(33)

Οὐδ' ἀργυρέη κω τότ' ἔλαμπε πειθώ.

Nor then did Persuasion yet shine silver-handed.

XXI

(36)

Αἰνοπαθῆ πατρίδ' ἐπόψομαι.

I shall look upon my sore-stricken father land.

XXII

(38)

Ἀσήμων ὑπὲρ ἑρμάτων φορεῦμαι.

Over hidden reefs I am borne.

XXIII

(41)

Ὁ Μεγίστης δ' ὁ φιλόφρων δέκα δὴ μῆνες, ἐπεί τε
στεφανοῦταί τε λύγῳ καὶ τρύγα πίνει μελιηδέα.

Ten months it is since Megistes, the gentle-hearted, was wreathed with willow, and drank the sweet vintage-wine.

XXIV

(42)

Καθαρῇ δ' ἐν κελέβῃ πέντε τε καὶ τρεῖς ἀναχείσθων.

In a spotless bowl let there be mixed five measures of water and three of wine.

XXV
(43)

Πολιοὶ μὲν ἡμὶν ἤδη κρόταφοι κάρη τε λευκόν,
χαρίεσσα δ' οὐκέθ' ἥβη πάρα, γηράλεοι δ' ὀδόντες.
γλυκεροῦ δ' οὐκέτι πολλὸς βιότου χρόνος λέλειπται·
διὰ ταῦτ' ἀνασταλύζω θαμὰ Τάρταρον δεδοικώς.
Ἀίδεω γάρ ἐστι δεινὸς μυχός, ἀργαλέη δ' ἐς αὐτόν
κάθοδος· καὶ γὰρ ἑτοῖμον καταβάντι μὴ ἀναβῆναι.

Now are my temples grey, and my head white, and gracious youth is no longer with me, and my teeth are old. And a long time of sweet life is no more left me; wherefore I often sigh in fear of Tartarus. For terrible is the depth of Hades, and grievous the descent to it; for it is fated for him that has gone down to come not up again.

XXVI
(44)

Ἔραμαι (δέ) τοι συνηβᾶν· χαριτεῦν ἔχεις γὰρ ἦθος.

I long to take joy with thee, for thou hast a pleasant soul.

XXVII
(45)

Ἐμὲ γὰρ (νέοι) λόγων εἵνεκα παῖδες ἂν φιλοῖεν·
χαρίεντα μὲν γὰρ ᾄδω, χαρίεντα δ' οἶδα λέξαι.

For the young would love me for my words, since sweetly I sing, and sweetly know how to speak.

XXVIII
(46)

'Αστραγάλαι δ' "Ερωτός εἰσιν μανίαι τε καὶ κύδοιμοι.

Love's dice are madnesses and tumults.

XXIX
(47)

Μεγάλῳ δηῦτέ μ' "Ερως ἔκοψεν ὥστε χαλκεὺς
πελέκει, χειμερίῃ δ' ἔλουσεν ἐν χαράδρῃ.

Love, like a smith, smites me again with a mighty axe, and bathes me in a stream winter-cold.

XXX
(48)

'Απέκειρας δ' ἁπαλῆς κόμης ἄμωμον ἄνθος.

Thou art shorn of the perfect flower of thy soft tresses.

XXXI
(50)

'Από μοι θανεῖν γένοιτ'· οὐ γὰρ ἂν ἄλλη
λύσις ἐκ πόνων γένοιτ' οὐδαμὰ τῶνδε.

Would that it might be mine to die, for no other release could there be in any wise from these troubles.

XXXII

(51)

Ἀγανῶς οἷά τε νεβρὸν νεοθηλέα
γαλαθηνόν, ὅστ' ἐν ὕλης κεροέσσης
ἀπολειφθεὶς ὑπὸ μητρὸς ἐπτοήθη.

Gently as a new-born fawn unweaned, which, left by its antlered dam, quivers for fear in the woods.

XXXIII

(54)

Ἐπὶ δ' ὀφρύσιν σελίνων στεφανίσκους
θέμενοι θάλειαν ὁρτὴν ἀγάγωμεν
Διονύσῳ.

Placing wreaths of parsley upon our brows, let us lead the goodly festival to Dionysus.

XXXIV

(62)

Φέρ' ὕδωρ, φέρ' οἶνον, ὦ παῖ,
φέρε δ' ἀνθεμεῦντας ἡμίν
στεφάνους, ἔνεικον, ὡς δὴ
πρὸς Ἔρωτα πυκταλίζω.

Bring water, bring wine, O boy, bring garlands of flowers to us, hither with them, that I may try a boxing-match with Love.

XXXV

(63)

Ἄγε δή, φέρ' ἡμίν, ὦ παῖ,
κελέβην, ὅκως ἄμυστιν
προπίω, τὰ μὲν δέκ' ἐγχέας
ὕδατος, τὰ πέντε δ' οἴνου
κυάθους, ὡς ἀνυβριστί
ἀνὰ δηῦτε βασσαρήσω.

* * *

Ἄγε δηῦτε μηκέθ' οὕτω
πατάγῳ τε κἀλαλητῷ
Σκυθικὴν πόσιν παρ' οἴνῳ
μελετῶμεν, ἀλλὰ καλοῖς
ὑποπίνοντες ἐν ὕμνοις.

Come, bring to us a goblet, boy, for me to drink a long health, and pour in ten measures of water and five of wine, that I may revel again without turbulence.

* * * * * *

How now, let us no longer thus with din and uproar practise Scythian drinking at our cups, but quaffing little, with goodly singing the while.

XXXVI

(65)

Τὸν Ἔρωτα γὰρ τὸν ἁβρὸν
μέλομαι βρύοντα μίτραις
πολυανθέμοις ἀείδειν·

ὅδε γὰρ θεῶν δυναστής,
ὅδε καὶ βροτοὺς δαμάζει.

For it is my care to sing of delicate Love, decked with garlands of many a flower; since he is lord of the gods, and he vanquishes men also.

XXXVII

(68)

Μνᾶται δηὖτε φαλακρὸς Ἄλεξις.

Bald-pate Alexis goes again a-wooing.

XXXVIII

(70)

Ὀρσόλοπος μὲν Ἄρης φιλέει μεναίχμαν.

Fiery Ares loves the man staunch in fight.

XXXIX

(72)

Νῦν δ' ἀπὸ μὲν στέφανος πόλεος ὄλωλεν.

But now has the city's crown of towers perished.

XL

(74)

... Ἐγὼ δὲ μισέω
πάντας, ὅσοι χθονίους ἔχουσι ῥυσμούς
καὶ χαλεπούς· μεμάθηκά σ', ὦ Μεγίστη,
τῶν ἀβακιζομένων.

I hate all that have a temper secret and stern, but I have found thee, O Megistes, to be of the gentle-minded.

XLI

(75)

In Puellam Immaturam et Fugacem

Πῶλε Θρῃκίη, τί δή με λοξὸν ὄμμασιν βλέπουσα
νηλεῶς φεύγεις, δοκέεις δέ μ' οὐδὲν εἰδέναι σοφόν·
ἴσθι τοι, καλῶς μὲν ἄν τοι τὸν χαλινὸν ἐμβάλοιμι,
ἡνίας δ' ἔχων στρέφοιμί σ' ἀμφὶ τέρματα δρόμου.
νῦν δὲ λειμῶνάς τε βόσκεαι κοῦφά τε σκιρτῶσα
  παίζεις·
δεξιὸν γὰρ ἱπποσείρην οὐκ ἔχεις ἐπεμβάτην.

Thracian filly, why, looking upon me with eyes askance, dost thou pitilessly fly me, and deem that I know naught of wisdom? Be sure that I would deftly place a bit upon thee, and, reins in hand, would wheel thee round the midway pillar of the course. But now thou grazest over the meadows, and lightly bounding dost take thy sport, for thou hast no skilful, steed-curbing rider.

XLII
(76)

Κλῦθί μευ γέροντος εὐέθειρα χρυσόπεπλε κούρα.

Maiden of the fair tresses and golden robe, give ear to me that am old.

XLIII
(77)

Εὖτέ μοι λευκαὶ μελαίναις ἀναμεμίξονται τρίχες.

When white hairs shall have been mingled with my black.

XLIV
(83)

Στεφάνους δ' ἀνὴρ τρεῖς ἕκαστος εἶχεν,
τοὺς μὲν ῥοδίνους, τὸν δὲ Ναυκρατίτην.

And each man had three garlands, two of roses and one of the myrtle of Naucratis.

XLV
(84)

Ἔστε ξένοισι μειλίχοις ἐοικότες,
στέγης τε μοῦνον καὶ πυρὸς κεχρημένοις.

Ye are like to gentle strangers needing only shelter and fire.

XLVI

(85)

Πάλαι ποτ' ἦσαν ἄλκιμοι Μιλήσιοι.

Once of old there were brave Milesians.

XLVII

(88)

Κοὐ μοκλὸν ἐν θύρῃσι διξῇσιν βαλών
ἥσυχος καθεύδει.

And without shooting the bolt in the double doors, he sleeps quietly.

XLVIII

(89)

Ἐρῶ τε δηὖτε κοὐκ ἐρῶ
καὶ μαίνομαι κοὐ μαίνομαι.

I love again and love not, I am mad and then not mad.

XLIX

(90)

Μηδ' ὥστε κῦμα πόντιον
λάλαζε, τῇ πολυκρότῃ
σὺν Γαστροδώρῃ καταχύδην
πίνουσα τὴν ἐπίστιον.

Babble not like a wave of the sea, while with

noisy Gastrodore you drain without measure the cup to the hearth-gods.

L.
(92)
Ὁ μὲν θέλων μάχεσθαι,
πάρεστι γάρ, μαχέσθω.

He that has a mind to fight, let him fight, for now is the time.

LI
(93)
Ὦ 'ραννὲ δὴ λίην,
πολλοῖσι γὰρ μέλεις.

O boy too fair, for thou art loved of many.

LII
(114)
Ἀλκίμων σ', ὠριστοκλείδη, πρῶτον οἰκτείρω φίλων,
ὤλεσας δ' ἥβην, ἀμύνων πατρίδος δουληΐην.

First of my valiant friends I mourn thee, Aristocleides, who didst lose thy young life, warding off slavery from thy country.

SIMONIDES

Simonides (556-467 B.C.) is a link between two very different periods of Greek history, the one which preceded, and the one which followed the Persian wars, and played throughout an important part amongst his contemporaries. He was born an Ionian in the island of Ceos, lived under the protection of Hipparchus at Athens, afterwards with the great Thessalian families of the Aleuadae and Scopadae, returned to Athens shortly after the close of the second Persian war, and removed soon afterwards to the court of Hiero, the tyrant of Syracuse, where he was a rival and enemy of Pindar. He remained in Sicily till the time of his death. He was the first to make use of lyric poetry as a means of addressing a national audience upon national themes, and also the first to make a practice of commemorating special occasions for a money fee.

I
(4)

Τῶν ἐν Θερμοπύλαις θανόντων
εὐκλεὴς μὲν ἁ τύχα, καλὸς δ' ὁ πότμος,
βωμὸς δ' ὁ τάφος, πρὸ γόων δὲ μνᾶστις, ὁ δ' οἶκτος
  ἔπαινος·
ἐντάφιον δὲ τοιοῦτον οὔτ' εὐρὼς
οὔθ' ὁ πανδαμάτωρ ἀμαυρώσει χρόνος.

ἀνδρῶν ἀγαθῶν ὅδε σηκὸς οἰκέταν εὐδοξίαν
Ἑλλάδος εἵλετο· μαρτυρεῖ δὲ καὶ Λεωνίδας
Σπάρτας βασιλεύς, ἀρετᾶς μέγαν λελοιπὼς
κόσμον ἀέναον κλέος τε.

Of those that died in Thermopylae glorious is the fortune, and fair the doom; their grave is an altar; for mourning they have remembrance, for lamentation praise. And such a winding-sheet neither decay nor all-conquering time shall make dim.

This sepulchre of valiant men has received the fair fame of Hellas for its habitant, as Leonidas also, king of Sparta, bears witness, who has left behind great glory of noble deeds and renown ever fresh.

II

(5)

This poem is addressed to Simonides' patron, Scopas of Thessaly, a man of notoriously bad character, whom the poet adroitly avoids censuring.

Ἄνδρ' ἀγαθὸν μὲν ἀλαθέως γενέσθαι
χαλεπὸν χερσίν τε καὶ ποσὶ καὶ νόῳ τετράγωνον,
    ἄνευ ψόγου τετυγμένον·
ὃς ἄν ᾖ κακὸς μηδ' ἄγαν ἀπάλαμνος, εἰδώς γ' ὀνασί-
    πολιν δίκαν
ὑγιὴς ἀνήρ· οὐδὲ μή μιν ἐγώ
μωμάσομαι· τῶν γὰρ ἀλιθίων
ἀπείρων γενέθλα.
πάντα τοι καλά, τοῖσί τ' αἰσχρὰ μὴ μέμικται.

Οὐδέ μοι ἐμμελέως τὸ Πιττάκειον
νέμεται, καίτοι σοφοῦ παρὰ φωτὸς εἰρημένον· χαλε-
    πὸν φάτ' ἐσθλὸν ἔμμεναι.
θεὸς ἂν μόνος τοῦτ' ἔχοι γέρας· ἄνδρα δ' οὐκ ἔστι
    μὴ οὐ κακὸν ἔμμεναι,
ὃν ἀμάχανος συμφορὰ καθέλῃ.
πράξαις γὰρ εὖ πᾶς ἀνὴρ ἀγαθός,
κακὸς δ', εἰ κακῶς (τι)·
καὶ τὸ πλεῖστον ἄριστοι, τοὺς θεοὶ φιλέωντι.

Τοὔνεκεν οὔποτ' ἐγὼ τὸ μὴ γενέσθαι
δυνατὸν διζήμενος, κενεὰν ἐς ἄπρακτον ἐλπίδα μοῖραν
    αἰῶνος βαλέω,
πανάμωμον ἄνθρωπον, εὐρυέδους ὅσοι καρπὸν αἰνύ-
    μεθα χθονός·
ἐπί τ' ὕμμιν εὑρὼν ἀπαγγελέω.

πάντας δ' ἐπαίνημι καὶ φιλέω,
ἑκὼν ὅστις ἔρδῃ
μηδὲν αἰσχρόν, ἀνάγκᾳ δ' οὐδὲ θεοὶ μάχονται

It is difficult for a man to become truly good, perfect as a square in hands and feet and mind, wrought without blame. Whosoever is not evil nor beyond measure worthless, who takes thought for justice, the upholder of cities, is a sound man. Verily, I will not blame him, for the race of fools is endless. All things, in truth, are good, in which baseness is not mixed.

Nor do I deem the words of Pittacus to have been fitly spoken, though from the mouth of a wise man. 'Hard,' he said, 'it is to be good.' Nay, this glory god alone would have, but a man cannot but be bad whom resistless misfortune seizes. For every one is good who has fared well, but bad if he has in aught fared ill, and for the most part those are best whom the gods love.

Wherefore never will I cast away my portion of life idly upon a bootless hope, seeking for that which cannot be, a man wholly without blame amongst all of us that eat the fruits of the broad-seated earth; when I have found such an one, I will declare him to you. But I praise and love all who of their own will do nothing base; but against necessity not even the gods contend.

III

(7)

From an Epinicion in honour of mules, only one side of whose parentage is referred to.

Χαίρετ' ἀελλοπόδων θύγατρες ἵππων.

Hail, daughters of storm-swift steeds.

IV

(8)

Glaucus the Boxer

Οὐδὲ Πολυδεύκεος βία
χεῖρας ἀντείναιτ' ἂν ἐναντίον αὐτῷ,
οὐδὲ σιδάρεον 'Αλκμάνας τέκος.

Neither mighty Pollux, nor Alcmene's iron son, would lift hands against him.

V

(10)

Astylus the Runner

Τίς δὴ τῶν γε νῦν τοσάσδε πέταλσι μύρτων
ἢ στεφάνοισι ῥόδων ἀνεδήσατο νίκας
ἐν ἀγῶνι περικτιόνων;

Who of men now living garlanded so many victories, with leaves of myrtle or chaplets of the rose, in the contest of the country-side?

VI

(12)

Ὡς ὁπόταν χειμέριον κατὰ μῆνα πινύσκῃ
Ζεὺς ἄματα τέσσαρα καὶ δέκα,
λαθάνεμόν τέ μιν ὥραν καλέοισιν ἐπιχθόνιοι
ἱρὰν παιδοτρόφον ποικίλας
ἀλκυόνος.

As when in the winter month Zeus brings fourteen days of calm, and mortals call it the sacred, windless breeding-time of the many-coloured halcyon.

VII

(13)

A pun upon the name of a defeated athlete, Crius (κριός, a ram).

Ἐπέξαθ' ὁ Κριὸς οὐκ ἀεικέως
ἐλθὼν ἐς εὐδενδρον ἀγλαὸν Διὸς
τέμενος.

Fittingly did Crius lose his fleece, when he came to the glorious tree-planted precinct of Zeus.

VIII

(14)

Πῖνε, πῖν' ἐπὶ συμφοραῖς.

Drink, drink to the good hap.

IX
(25)
Wind at Sea

Ἁπαλὺς δ' ὑπὲρ κυμάτων χεύμενος
πορφύρεα σχίζει περὶ πρώραν τὰ κύματα.

And streaming softly over the billows it parts the dark-gleaming waves about the prow.

X
(29)

This and the following fragment refer to the movements of a chorus in the dance.

Ἀπέλαστον ἵππον ἢ κύνα
Ἀμυκλαίαν ἀγωνίῳ
ἐλελιζόμενος ποδὶ μίμεο, καμπύλον μέλος διώκων.

Show thyself like a horse that none can outstrip, or a hound of Amyclae, thy feet whirling in the contest, as thou followest the mazy strain.

XI
(30)

Οἷος (δὲ κύων) ἀνὰ Δώτιον ἀνθεμόεν πεδίον
πέταται θάνατον κεροέσσᾳ
εὑρέμεν ματεύων ἐλάφῳ·
τὰν μεθέπ' αὐχένα στρέφοισαν ὑγρόν τε κάρα
πάντ' ἐπ' οἶμον.

And as a dog courses over the flower-bearing plain of Dotium, seeking to bring death to an antlered hind, and pursues it as it turns every way its neck and supple head.

XII
(31)

Ὄπα δὲ γαρῦσαι
σύν τ' ἐλαφρὸν ὄρχημα οἶδα ποδῶν μιγνύμεν·[1]
Κρῆτά μιν καλέοισι τρόπον, τό τ' ὄργανον Μολοσσόν.

I know how to lift the voice in song, and to join therewith the light tripping of the feet; Cretan they call the mode, and the instrument the Molossian.

XIII
(32)

The reference is to the fall of the Scopadae.

Ἄνθρωπος ἐὼν μή ποτε φάσῃς ὅ τι γίνεται αὔριον,
μηδ' ἄνδρα ἰδὼν ὄλβιον, ὅσσον χρόνον ἔσσεται·
ὠκεῖα γάρ, οὐδὲ τανυπτερύγου μυίας
οὐ τόσα μετάστασις.

Never say, being mortal, what comes to pass to-morrow, nor when thou seest a man happy, for how long time he will be so. For swift is the transit, and not so swift is that of the fly upon the wing.

[1] The first two lines as in Schneidewin's text.

XIV
(36)

Οὐδὲ γὰρ οἳ πρότερόν ποτ' ἐπέλοντο,
θεῶν δ' ἐξ ἀνάκτων ἐγένονθ' υἷες ἡμίθεοι,
ἄπονον οὐδ' ἄφθιτον οὐδ' ἀκίνδυνον βίον
ἐς γῆρας ἐξίκοντο τελέσσαντες.

For not even they who were before, the progeny half-divine of gods who were kings, not even did they reach old age fulfilling their life without toil or decay or perils.

XV
(37)

Danae

Ὅτε λάρνακι κεῖτ' ἐν δαιδαλέᾳ
ἄνεμός τ' ἐφόρει μιν πνέων κινηθεῖσά τε λίμνα,
δεῖμα προσεῖρπε τότ' οὐκ ἀδιάντοισι παρειαῖς,
ἀμφί τε Περσέϊ βάλλε φίλαν χέρ', εἶπέν τ'· ὦ τέκος,
οἷον ἔχω πόνον· σὺ δ' ἀωτεῖς·
γαλαθηνῷ λάθεϊ κνώσσεις ἐν ἀτερπεῖ
δούρατι χαλκεογόμφῳ,
νυκτὶ ἀλαμπεῖ κυανέῳ τε δνόφῳ καταλείς·
ἅλμαν δ' ὕπερθεν τεᾶν κομᾶν βαθεῖαν
παριόντος κύματος οὐκ ἀλέγεις, οὐδ' ἀνέμων
φθόγγον, πορφυρέᾳ
κείμενος ἐν χλανίδι, πρόσωπον κλιθὲν προσώπῳ.
εἰ δέ τοι δεινὸν τό γε δεινὸν ἦν,
καί κεν ἐμῶν ῥημάτων λεπτὸν ὑπεῖχες οὖας.

κέλομαι δ', εὖδε βρέφος, εὑδέτω δὲ πόντος,
εὑδέτω δ' ἄμοτον κακόν·
μεταιβολία δέ τις φανείη, Ζεῦ πάτερ,
ἐκ σέθεν· ὅττι δὲ θαρσαλέον ἔπος
εὔχομαι νόσφιν δίκας, σύγγνωθί μοι.

When she lay in the fair-wrought chest, and the wind with its breath and the troubled waters were bearing her, then terror crept upon her cheeks wet with tears, and casting her hand about Perseus, she said, 'O child, what woe is mine, but thou slumberest; with a babe's forgetfulness thou sleepest in a joyless barque brass-riveted, folded in with sunless night and black darkness. And thou heedest not the deep briny water of the wave passing above thy hair, nor the voice of the winds, as thou liest in thy purple cloak, thy cheek leaning against mine. Yet, if the terrible had terrors for thee, thou wouldst even turn a quick ear to my words. But I charge thee, sleep, little one, and let the sea sleep, and let our unceasing ills have sleep. And may some change appear, father Zeus, from thee; and in that I pray with bold words unlawfully, grant me pardon.'

XVI
(38)

Πάντα γὰρ μίαν ἱκνεῖται δασπλῆτα Χάρυβδιν,
αἱ μεγάλαι τ' ἀρεταὶ καὶ ὁ πλοῦτος.

For to one dread gulf come all things, both great virtues and wealth.

XVII

(39)

Ἀνθρώπων ὀλίγον μὲν κάρτος, ἄπρακτοι δὲ μεληδόνες
αἰῶνι δὲ παύρῳ πόνος ἀμφὶ πόνῳ·
ὁ δ' ἄφυκτος ὁμῶς ἐπικρέμαται θάνατος·
κείνου γὰρ ἴσον λάχον μέρος οἵ τ' ἀγαθοί
ὅστις τε κακός.

Little is the might of men, and bootless their cares, and in a brief life there is trouble upon trouble. And death, not to be escaped, hangs over all alike; for of that both the good, and whosoever is bad, have won an equal share.

XVIII

(40)

Orpheus

Τοῦ καὶ ἀπειρέσιοι ποτῶντο
ὄρνιθες ὑπὲρ κεφαλᾶς, ἀνὰ δ' ἰχθύες ὀρθοί
κυανέου ἐξ ὕδατος ἄλλοντο καλᾷ σὺν ἀοιδᾷ.

Over whose head there also flew birds unnumbered, and fishes leapt upright from the dark water at the goodly strain.

XIX

(41)

Οὐδὲ γὰρ ἐννοσίφυλλος ἀήτα τότ' ὦρτ' ἀνέμων,
ἅ τις κατεκώλυε κιδναμέναν μελιαδέα γᾶρυν
ἀραρεῖν ἀκουαῖσι βροτῶν.

For no leaf-shaking gale of winds did then

arise, that hindered the spreading, tuneful voice from meeting the ears of men.

XX
(42)

'Ρεῖα θεοὶ κλέπτοισιν ἀνθρώπων νόον.

Easily do the gods beguile the mind of mortals.

XXI
(43)
Love

Σχέτλιε παῖ, δολόμητις Ἀφροδίτα
τὸν Ἄρει κακομαχάνῳ τέκεν.

Cruel-hearted boy, whom guileful Aphrodite bore to mischief-working Ares.

XXII
(45)
Musarum Fons

Ἁγνὰ ἐπίσκοπε Κλειοῖ, χερνίβων πολύλιστον
ἅτ' ἀρυόντεσσι νᾶμα χρυσοπέπλου Μναμοσύνας
εὐῶδες ἵεις ἀμβροσίων ἐκ μυχῶν ἐραννὸν ὕδωρ.

Holy, guardian Clio that from the divine hollow sendest forth a fair fragrant stream for those drawing from golden-robed Mnemosyne's lustral fount, sought with many a prayer.

XXIII
(46)

Ἀ Μοῖσα γὰρ οὐκ ἀπόρως γεύει τὸ παρὸν μόνον, ἀλλ'
ἐπέρχεται
πάντα θεριζομένα· μή μοι καταπαύετ', ἐπείπερ ἄρξατο
τερπνοτάτων μελέων ὁ καλλιβόας πολύχορδος αὐλός.

For the Muse gives not men to taste in meagre fashion only of that which is before them, but goes onward, gathering all things to her harvest. Prithee, stay her not, since the fair-sounding flute of many notes has begun its strains most sweet.

XXIV
(47)

Ὁμιλεῖ δ' ἄνθεσιν, (ὧτε) μέλισσα
ξανθὸν μέλι μηδομένα.

But the poet dwells amid flowers, like a bee busied with golden honey.

XXV
(51)

Ἴσχει δέ με πορφυρέας
ἁλὸς ἀμφιταρασσομένας ὀρυμαγδός.

And the roar of the dark-gleaming sea, tossing round about, enfolds me.

XXVI

(52)

(Εὐρυδίκας)
ἰοστεφάνου γλυκεῖαν ἐδάκρυσαν
ψυχὰν ἀποπνέοντα γαλαθηνὸν τέκος.

They wept for the babe unweaned of violet-crowned Eurydice, when he breathed forth his sweet life.

XXVII

(53)

Meleager

"Ὃς δουρὶ πάντας
νίκασε νέους δινάεντα βαλών
"Ἄναυρον ὕπερ πολυβότρυος ἐξ Ἰωλκοῦ·
οὕτω γὰρ Ὅμηρος ἠδὲ Στασίχορος ἄεισε λαοῖς.

Who outdid all the young men with the spear, hurling it from vine-clad Iolcus beyond the eddying Anaurus; for so sang Homer and Stesichorus to the peoples.

XXVIII

(55)

Βίοτον κέ σε μᾶλλον ὤνασα πρότερος ἐλθών.

Had I come earlier, I would have better given thee the boon of life.

XXIX
(57)

A criticism of the epigram by Cleobulus, one of the seven sages, upon the funeral monument of Midas.

Τίς κεν αἰνήσειε νόῳ πίσυνος Λίνδου ναέταν Κλεό-
βουλον
ἀενάοις ποταμοῖς ἄνθεσί τ' εἰαρινοῖσιν
ἀελίου τε φλογὶ χρυσέᾳ λιπαρᾶς τε σελάνας
καὶ θαλασσίαισι δίναις ἀντία θέντα μένος στάλας;
ἅπαντα γάρ ἐστι θεῶν ἥσσω· λίθον δὲ
καὶ βρότεοι παλάμαι θραύοντι· μωροῦ φωτὸς ἅδε
βουλά.

Who that is wise in mind would praise Cleobulus, the dweller in Lindus, who likened the might of a pillar to the ever-flowing rivers, and the flowers of spring, and the golden beams of the sun and of the shining moon, and the eddies of the sea? For all things are subject to the gods, and as for stone the hands also of mortals shatter it. Behold in this the thought of a foolish man.

XXX
(58)

Ἔστι τις λόγος ποτὲ τὰν ἀρετάν
ναίειν δυσαμβάτοις ἐπὶ πέτραις,
νῦν δέ μιν θεῶν χῶρον ἁγνὸν ἀμφέπειν,
οὐδ' ἁπαντᾶν βλεφάροις θνατῶν ἔσοπτον,

ᾇ μὴ δακέθυμος ἱδρώς
ἔνδοθεν μόλῃ θ', ἵκηταί τ' ἐς ἄκρον
ἀνδρείας.

There is a story that once virtue dwelt upon pathless rocks, but that now she guards the holy place of the gods, and meets not in visible presence the eyes of any mortals, save him from whose inmost frame comes heart-grieving sweat, and who reaches the topmost height of manhood.

XXXI

(60)

Ὤνθρωπε, κεῖσαι ζῶν ἔτι μᾶλλον τῶν ὑπὸ γᾶς ἐκείνων.

Fellow, while living thou art sunk in death, even more than those that are beneath the earth.

XXXII

(61)

Οὔτις ἄνευ θεῶν
ἀρετὰν λάβεν, οὐ πόλις, οὐ βροτός.
Θεὸς ὁ πάμμητις· ἀπήμαντον δέ
οὐδέν ἐστιν ἐν αὐτοῖς.

No one without the help of the gods wins virtue, neither man nor city. God is the all-contriving; but amongst mortals there is nothing free from pain.

XXXIII
(62)

Οὐκ ἔστιν κακὸν
ἀνεπιδόκητον ἀνθρώποις, ὀλίγῳ δὲ χρόνῳ
πάντα μεταρρίπτει θεός.

There is no evil not to be looked for by men, and in a little time god overturns all things.

XXXIV
(65)

Ὁ δ' αὖ θάνατος κίχε καὶ τὸν φυγόμαχον.

Death comes also to him who flies from the fight.

XXXV
(66)

Ἔστι καὶ σιγᾶς ἀκίνδυνον γέρας.

Silence too has its safe reward.

XXXVI
(67)

Πόλις ἄνδρα διδάσκει.

Statecraft instructs a man.

XXXVII
(68)

Ἐπεὶ
πάσαις κορυδαλλίσι χρὴ λόφον ἐγγενέσθαι.

Since on every crested lark a crest there must be.

XXXVIII
(69)

Τὸ γὰρ γεγενημένον οὐκέτ' ἄρεκτον ἔσται.

For that which has come to pass will no more be a thing unfulfilled.

XXXIX
(70)

Οὐδὲ καλᾶς σοφίας ἐστὶν χάρις,
εἰ μή τις ἔχει σεμνὰν ὑγίειαν.

Nor is there grace in fair wisdom, unless one has health the divine.

XL
(71)

Τίς γὰρ ἀδονᾶς ἄτερ
θνατῶν βίος ποθεινὸς ἢ ποία τυραννίς;
τᾶς δ' ἄτερ οὐδὲ θεῶν ζαλωτὸς αἰών.

For what life of mortals, or what tyranny, is desirable, if void of pleasure? Without that not even the estate of the gods is to be envied.

XLI
(72)

Πορφυρέου
ἀπὸ στόματος ἱεῖσα φωνὰν παρθένος.

A maiden breathing forth her voice from rosy lips.

XLII

(73)

Εὖτ' ἀηδόνες πολυκώτιλοι,
χλωραύχενες, εἰαριναί.

When the yellow-throated, carolling nightingales, birds of spring . . .

XLIII

(74)

Ἄγγελε κλυτὰ ἔαρος ἁδυόδμου,
κυανέα χελιδοῖ.

Dark swallow, goodly messenger of sweet-scented spring.

XLIV

(75)

The reference is perhaps to words uttered by Pindar on an occasion when he had defeated Simonides in a poetical contest.

Κούρων δ' ἐξελέγχει νέος
οἶνος οὐ τὸ πέρυσι δῶρον
ἀμπέλου· ὁ δὲ μῦθος κενεόφρων.

The new wine of boys puts not to shame last year's gift of the vine, but the saying is a foolish one.

XLV
(76)

Τὸ δοκεῖν καὶ τὰν ἀλάθειαν βιᾶται.

Seeming o'ermasters even truth.

XLVI
(77)

Μόνος ἅλιος ἐν οὐρανῷ.

The sun reigns alone in the sky.

TIMOCREON

Timocreon was a Rhodian aristocrat, banished from his country on a charge, the truth of which he himself confesses in Frag. iii., of medising. He made in Athens the acquaintance of Themistocles, and became a bitter enemy of his for the reasons set forth in Frag. i. There was also a personal hostility between Timocreon and Simonides.

TIMOCREON

I

(1)

Ἀλλ' εἰ τύγε Παυσανίαν ἢ καὶ τύγε Ξάνθιππον
   αἰνέεις
ἢ τύγε Λευτυχίδαν, ἐγὼ δ' Ἀριστείδαν ἐπαινέω
ἄνδρ' ἱερᾶν ἀπ' Ἀθανᾶν
ἐλθεῖν ἕνα λῷστον, ἐπεὶ Θεμιστοκλῆ' ἤχθαρε Λατώ,
ψεύσταν, ἄδικον, προδόταν, ὃς Τιμοκρέοντα ξεῖνον
   ἐόντα
ἀργυρίοισι κυβαλικοῖσι πεισθεὶς οὐ κατᾶγεν
ἐς πατρίδ' Ἰάλυσον·
λαβὼν δὲ τρί' ἀργυρίου τάλαντ' ἔβα πλέων εἰς
   ὄλεθρον,
τοὺς μὲν κατάγων ἀδίκως, τοὺς δ' ἐκδιώκων, τοὺς δὲ
   καίνων,
ἀργυρίων ὑπόπλεως· Ἰσθμοῖ δ' ἐπανδόκευε γλοιῶς
ψυδρὰ κρέα παρέχων·
οἱ δ' ἤσθιον κηὔχοντο μὴ ὤραν Θεμιστοκλέος γενέσθαι.

The allusion in the concluding lines is probably to a division of the spoil exacted from medising cities, in which Themistocles took the lion's share.

But if you praise Pausanias, or you Xanthippus, or you Leutychides, I extol Aristides as the one best man that came from sacred Athens, since upon Themistocles Leto looked with loathing, a man false, unjust, and traitorous, who won by base bribes restored not his own friend Timocreon to his native Ialysus. But having received three talents of silver he departed on a baneful voyage, restoring some unjustly, and casting some forth, and slaying some, loading himself with secret gains. And at the Isthmus he made miserly entertainment, furnishing counterfeit meats; and the rest did eat, and prayed that Themistocles' harvest-time might never come.

II
(2)

The beginning of a poem attacking Themistocles after his fall. The reference is the same in the next fragment.

Μοῦσα, τοῦδε τοῦ μέλεος
κλέος ἀν' Ἕλλανας τίθει,
ὡς ἐοικὸς καὶ δίκαιον.

Muse, set forth the fame of this song among the Greeks, as is fitting and just.

III
(3)

Οὐκ ἄρα Τιμοκρέων μοῦνος
Μήδοισιν ὡρκιατόμει,
ἀλλ' ἐντὶ κἄλλοι δὴ πονηροί·
οὐκ ἐγὼ μόνα κόλουρις·
ἐντὶ καὶ ἄλλαι ἀλώπεκες.

It was not, then, Timocreon alone that made a league with the Medes, but there are other scoundrels as well; I am not the only one without a tail,—there are other foxes besides.

IV
(8)

Ὠφελέν σ', ὦ τυφλὲ Πλοῦτε, μήτε γῇ μήτ' ἐν
θαλάσσῃ μήτ' ἐν ἠπείρῳ φανῆμεν,
ἀλλὰ Τάρταρόν τε ναίειν κἀχέροντα· διὰ σὲ γὰρ
σύμπαντ' ἐν ἀνθρώποις κακά.

Would that thou, blind God of wealth, hadst not appeared either on earth or sea or land, but didst inhabit Tartarus and Acheron; for all the evils amongst men are on account of thee.

V
(9)

Ὧι ξυμβουλεύειν χέρς ἄπο, νοῦς δὲ πάρα.

Whose mind is ready for counsel, but whose hand holds back.

VI
(10)

The reference is to the epigram of Simonides (Bergk, 170).

Μοῦσά μοι 'Αλκμήνης καλλισφύρου υἱὸν ἄειδε·
υἱὸν 'Αλκμήνης ἄειδε Μοῦσά μοι καλλισφύρου.

It is the opinion of Bergk that in these lines Simonides was himself ridiculing the style of Timocreon.

Κηΐα με προσῆλθε φλυαρία οὐκ ἐθέλοντα.
Οὐκ ἐθέλοντά με προσῆλθε Κηΐα φλυαρία.

The prating of the Cean came to my ears unacceptably. Unacceptably to my ears came the prating of the Cean.

CORINNA

A poetess of Tanagra in Boeotia. She and Myrtis, who also belonged to Boeotia, were elder contemporaries of Pindar, who was born in 521 B.C. They contended with and defeated Pindar in his early youth, and he is said to have received help and instruction in his art from Corinna.

I

(9)

Possibly the words of a divine visitant.

Ἦ διανεκῶς εὕδεις; οὐ μὰν πάρος ἦσθα Κόριννα.

Sleepest thou unceasingly? Yet before, Corinna, it was not so with thee.

II

(20)

Κλία γέροντ᾽ ἀϊσομένα
Ταναγρίδεσσι λευκοπέπλυς·
μέγα δ᾽ ἐμῆς γέγασε πόλις
λιγυροκωτίλης ἐνόπης.

To sing ancient glories to the white-robed women of Tanagra; and the city joys greatly in my voice clear-carolling.

III

(21)

Μέμφομη δὲ κὴ λιγουρὰν Μουρτίδ' ἰώνγα,
ὅτι βανὰ φοῦσ' ἔβα Πινδάροιο ποτ' ἔριν.

For my part I blame also tuneful Myrtis, that being a woman she set forth to vie with Pindar.

LAMPROCLES

A dithyrambic poet, belonging probably to the early part of the fifth century B.C.

I

(2)

The Pleiads

Αἴτε ποταναῖς
ὁμώνυμοι πελειάσιν αἰθέρι νεῖσθε.

Ye that move in the sky, of the same name with winged doves.

PRATINAS

Pratinas was a Dorian of Phlius in the northern Peloponnese, but is associated with Athens in the first part of the fifth century B.C. He competed with Aeschylus, and the first development of satyric drama, as distinct from tragedy proper, is ascribed to him. As a writer of dithyrambs, he appears in the first fragment as attacking the newer school of dithyrambists, who had abandoned the lyre for the flute, and who tended by their excessive attention to musical accompaniment to diminish the importance of the poet and chorus.

I

(1)

Τίς ὁ θόρυβος ὅδε; τί τάδε τὰ χορεύματα;
τίς ὕβρις ἔμολεν ἐπὶ Διονυσιάδα πολυπάταγα θυ-
    μέλαν;
ἐμὸς ἐμὸς ὁ Βρόμιος· ἐμὲ δεῖ κελαδεῖν, ἐμὲ δεῖ
    παταγεῖν
ἀν' ὄρεα θύμενον μετὰ Ναϊάδων
οἷά τε κύκνον ἄγοντα ποικιλόπτερον μέλος.
τὰν ἀοιδὰν κατέστασε Πιερὶς βασίλειαν· ὁ δ' αὐλός
ὕστερον χορενέτω· καὶ γάρ ἐσθ' ὑπηρέτας
κώμῳ μόνον θυραμάχοις τε πυγμαχίαισι νέων θέλει
    παροίνων
ἔμμεναι στρατηλατάς.
παῖε τὸν Φρύγα τὸν ἀοιδοῦ
ποικίλου προαχέοντα·
φλέγε τὸν ὀλεσισιαλοκάλαμον,
λαλοβαρυόπα παραμελορυθμοβάταν θ'
ὑπαὶ τρυπάνῳ δέμας πεπλασμένον.
ἠν ἰδού· ἅδε σοι δεξιά
καὶ ποδὸς διαρριφά, θριαμβοδιθύραμβε·
κισσόχαιτ' ἄναξ ἄκουε τὰν ἐμὰν Δώριον χορείαν.

What din is here? What dances are these?
What insolence has come to the oft-trodden stage
of Dionysus? The Bromian is mine, is mine; it
s for me to cry, for me to raise a clashing sound,

speeding over the mountains with the Naiads, and like a swan sending forth a melody of many-hued flight. The Pierian muse made the song supreme; let the flute be second in the dance, for it is servant; only in the revel and the door-assailing strifes of drunken striplings is it wont to be lord. Beat off the Phrygian whose notes take the lead of the well-skilled singer; burn the spittle-wasting, loud-babbling flute, that comes marring tune and measure, its body shaped beneath the boring-tool. Behold now, god of the dithyramb, like this are their right hands[1] and outflung feet; but do thou, ivy-crowned king, give ear to my Dorian strain.

II
(2)
Spartan love of Music

Λάκων ὁ τέττιξ εὔτυκος ἐς χορόν.

The grass-hopper of Lacedaemon is ready for the dance.

III
(3)

Οὐ γᾶν αὐλακισμέναν ἀρῶν, ἀλλ' ἄσκαφον ματεύων.

Ploughing not a land already furrowed, but seeking one untilled.

---

[1] The chorus here probably imitate derisively the action of the fingers up and down the stops of the flute.

PHRYNICHUS

This is the Athenian tragic poet of that name, who exhibited plays from about 512 to 476 B.C. A great share in the development of tragedy belongs to him, his chief excellence as a writer lying in the lyrical side of it.

I

(2)

Λάμπει δ' ἐπὶ πορφυρέαις παρῇσι φῶς ἔρωτος.

And on his glowing cheeks shines the light of love.

DIAGORAS

Diagoras was born in the island of Melos. The following dithyrambic fragment is curiously opposed to his subsequent speculations in philosophy, which procured for him the title of the Atheist, and led to his expulsion from Athens in 411 B.C. on a charge of impiety.

1

(1)

Θεός, θεὸς πρὸ παντὸς ἔργου βροτείου
νωμᾷ φρέν' ὑπερτάταν,
αὐτοδαὴς δ' ἀρετὰ βραχὺν οἶμον ἕρπει.

It is God, God who before every deed of mortals moves his most high will, but virtue self-taught creeps but a little way.

CYDIAS

A native of Hermione in Argolis, and belonging, perhaps, in date to the beginning of the fifth century B.C.

I

(1)

Εὐλαβεῦ δὲ μὴ κατέναντα λέοντος
νεβρὸς ἐλθὼν μοῖραν αἱρεῖσθαι κρεῶν.

Fawn that you are, beware; lest, coming face to face with a lion, you take upon yourself the doom of becoming his prey.[1]

[1] Or 'claim a share in the prey,' a proverbial saying in reference to a lion. The first rendering, however, is better suited to the context in Plato *Charm.* 155 D., where the passage is quoted, and is supported by Jowett's translation *ad loc.*

PRAXILLA

A poetess of Sicyon, whose *floruit* is assigned to 450 B.C. She was famous for her scolia, or banquet-songs, and the charming metre employed in Frag. III. was named after her.

I

(2)

The answer of Adonis when questioned in the under-world.

Κάλλιστον μὲν ἐγὼ λείπω φάος ἠελίοιο,
δεύτερον ἄστρα φαεινὰ σεληναίης τε πρόσωπον
ἠδὲ καὶ ὡραίους σικύους καὶ μῆλα καὶ ὄγχνας.

The fairest thing that I leave is the light of the sun, and the next the bright stars and face of the moon,—and also ripe cucumbers and apples and pears.

II

(3)

Ἀδμήτου λόγον, ὦ' ταῖρε, μαθὼν τοὺς ἀγαθοὺς φίλει·
τῶν δειλῶν δ' ἀπέχου, γνοὺς ὅτι δειλῶν ὀλίγα χάρις.

Friend, having learnt the tale of Admetus, do thou love the good, bu keep thyself from the vile, knowing that in them is little grace.

III

(5)

ὦ διὰ τῶν θυρίδων καλὸν ἐμβλέποισα,
παρθένε τὰν κεφαλάν, τὰ δ' ἔνερθε νύμφα.

O thou that lookest sweetly through the indow, maiden in thy face, and yet withal a edded bride.

BACCHYLIDES

Bacchylides (*circ.* 500-430 B.C.) was born in the island of Ceos, and was a nephew of Simonides. He lived with him at the court of Hiero, and shared his hostility towards Pindar.

I
(1)

Ὄλβιος, ᾧτε θεὸς μοῖράν τε καλῶν ἔπορεν
σύν τ' ἐπιζάλῳ τύχᾳ ἀφνειὸν βιοτὰν διάγειν·
οὐ γάρ τις ἐπιχθονίων πάντα γ' εὐδαίμων ἔφυ.

Happy is he to whomsoever God has given a portion of good things, and to lead a life of plenty with prosperous fortune; for no one of dwellers upon earth is born blessed in all things.

II
(2)

Ὀνατοῖσι μὴ φῦναι φέριστον,
μηδ' ἀελίου προσιδεῖν φέγγος·
ὄλβιος δ' οὐδεὶς βροτῶν πάντα χρόνον.

Not to have been born is best for mortals, and not to look upon the light of the sun; and no one among men is happy alway.

III
(3)

Παύροισι δὲ θνατῶν τὸν ἅπαντα χρόνον δαίμων
  ἔδωκεν[1]
πράσσοντας ἐν καιρῷ πολιοκρόταφον
γῆρας ἱκνεῖσθαι, πρὶν ἐγκύρσαι δύᾳ.

To few mortals has fortune granted that, faring well all their time, they should come to hoary-browed old age without first encountering grief.

IV
(4)

Ὡς δ' ἅπαξ εἰπεῖν, φρένα καὶ πυκινὰν κέρδος ἀνθρώπων βιᾶται.

And to speak once for all, gain overbears even the wise-hearted of men.

V
(6)

Hiero's victory at Olympia

Ξανθότριχα μὲν Φερένικον
Ἀλφεὸν παρ' εὐρυδίναν πῶλον ἀελλοδρόμον
εἶδε νικάσαντα.

He saw chestnut-maned Pherenicus, steed swift as the storm, conquer by the broad-eddying Alpheus.

---

[1] Bergk retains the corrupt τῷ δαίμονι δῶκεν.

VI
(7)
Corinth

Ὦ Πέλοπος λιπαρᾶς νάσου θεόδματοι πύλαι.

O god-built gates of the bright isle of Pelops.

VII
(9)

Νίκα γλυκύδωρος . . .
ἐν πολυχρύσῳ δ' Ὀλύμπῳ Ζηνὶ παρισταμένα κρίνει
τέλος
ἀθανάτοισί τε καὶ θνατοῖς ἀρετᾶς.

Victory, giver of sweet gifts, standing by the side of Zeus in gold-decked Olympus, awards the issue of well-doing to immortals and to mortals.

VIII
(11)

Αἰαῖ τέκος ἁμέτερον,
μεῖζον ἢ πενθεῖν ἐφάνη κακόν, ἀφθέγκτοισιν ἴσον.

Alas, my child, an evil has appeared too great for grief, like to those unutterable.

IX
(13)

Τίκτει δέ τε θνατοῖσιν εἰράνα μεγάλα
πλοῦτον καὶ μελιγλώσσων ἀοιδᾶν ἄνθεα,
δαιδαλέων τ' ἐπὶ βωμῶν θευῖσιν αἴθεσθαι βοῶν
ξανθᾷ φλογὶ μῆρα τανυτρίχων τε μήλων,
γυμνασίων τε νέοις αὐλῶν τε καὶ κώμων μέλειν.

' Ἐν δὲ σιδαροδέτοις πόρπαξιν αἰθᾶν
ἀραχνᾶν ἵστοι πέλονται·
ἐγχεά τε λογχωτὰ ξίφεά τ' ἀμφάκεα δάμναται εὐρώς·
χαλκεᾶν δ' οὐκ ἔστι σαλπίγγων κτύπος·
οὐδὲ συλᾶται μελίφρων ὕπνος ἀπὸ βλεφάρων,
ἁμὸν ὃς θάλπει κέαρ.
συμποσίων δ' ἐρατῶν βρίθοντ' ἀγυιαί, παιδικοί θ'
ὕμνοι φλέγονται.

Peace the mighty brings forth wealth for mortals and the flowers of honey-voiced lays, and makes the thigh-bones of oxen and long-haired sheep to be burnt in the ruddy flame upon carven altars in honour of the gods, and the young men to turn to the sports of the training-school, and to flutes and revels. And in the breastplates bound with iron are the webs of red-brown spiders, and rust overgrows the pointed spears and two-edged swords, and there is no din of brazen trumpets. Nor is sweet sleep, that makes glad our heart, snatched from the eyes. And the streets are thronged with goodly drinking-companies, and songs to boys burst forth.

X
(14)

Directed against an opposite opinion expressed by Pindar.

Ἕτερος ἐξ ἑτέρου σοφὸς τό τε πάλαι τό τε νῦν.
οὐδὲ γὰρ ῥᾷστον ἀρρήτων ἐπέων πύλας
ἐξευρεῖν.

Now as of old one man becomes wise from

another; for not very easy is it to find the gates of words heretofore unuttered.

XI
(19)

Εἷς ὅρος, μία δὲ βροτοῖς ἐστὶν εὐτυχίας ὁδός,
θυμὸν εἴ τις ἔχων ἀπενθῆ διατελεῖν δύναται βίον·
ὃς δὲ μυρίαν μενοινὰν ἀμφιπολεῖ φρενί,
τὸ δὲ παρ' ἆμάρ τε καὶ νύκτα μελλόντων χάριν
ἑὸν ἰάπτεται κέαρ,
ἀκάρπωτον ἔχει πόνον.

There is one aim, one path of happiness for mortals, if one can bring his life to a close, keeping an ungrieved mind. But he who nurses thousand-fold desire in his soul, and by day and night is vexed at heart for what is to come, has fruitless toil.

XII
(20)

Τί γὰρ ἐλαφρὸν ἔτ' ἔστ' ἄπραχθ' (ὧδ') ὀδυρόμενον δονεῖν
καρδίαν;

For what solace comes from thus idly mourning and disquieting the heart?

XIII
(21)

Πάντεσσι θνατοῖσι δαίμων ἐπέταξε πόνους ἄλλοισιν
ἄλλους.

Upon all men has fortune laid troubles, some upon this one, others upon that.

XIV

(22)

Λυδία μὲν γὰρ λίθος μανύει χρυσόν,
ἀνδρῶν δ' ἀρετὰν σοφίαν τε παγκρατὴς ἐλέγχει
ἀλάθεια.

For the Lydian touch-stone reveals gold, and all-powerful truth tests the worth and wisdom of men.

XV

(23)

Οὐχ ἕδρας ἔργον οὐδ' ἀμβολᾶς, ἀλλὰ χρυσαιγίδος Ἰτωνίας
χρὴ παρ' εὐδαίδαλον ναὸν ἐλθόντας ἁβρόν τι δεῖξαι.

It is not a time to sit or to delay, but we must go to the fair-wrought temple of Itonian Pallas of the golden aegis, and show to her some comely rite.

XVI

(24)

The Cottabus

Εὖτε τὴν ἀπ' ἀγκύλης ἵησι
τοῖσδε τοῖς νεανίαις
λευκὸν ἀντείνασα πῆχυν.

When from her bent hand she throws the cast for these young men, uplifting her white arm.

XVII
(25)

Ἡ καλὸς Θεόκριτος· οὐ μόνος ἀνθρώπων ἐρᾷς.

Said fair Theocritus: 'Thou art not the only one of men who loves.'

XVIII
(27)

Γλυκεῖ' ἀνάγκα
ἐσσυμενᾶν κυλίκων θάλπησι θυμόν,
Κύπρις ὥς· ἐλπὶς γὰρ αἰθύσσει φρένας

ἀμμιγνυμένα Διονυσίοισι δώροις,
ἀνδράσι θ' ὑψοτάτω πέμπει μερίμνας·
αὐτίχ' ὁ μὲν πόλεων κρήδεμνα λύει,
πᾶσι δ' ἀνθρώποις μοναρχήσειν δοκεῖ·

χρυσῷ δ' ἐλέφαντί τε μαρμαίροισιν οἶκοι,
πυροφόροι δὲ κατ' αἰγλάεντα (καρπόν)
νᾶες ἄγουσιν ἀπ' Αἰγύπτου, μέγιστον
πλοῦτον· ὣς πίνοντος ὁρμαίνει κέαρ.

The sweet tyranny of riotous cups fires the heart even as Aphrodite does. For hope, mingling with the gifts of Dionysus, stirs the soul, and urges the thoughts of a man to their highest. At once he overthrows the battlements of cities, and thinks he will be sole ruler over all men. Houses he has that flash with gold and ivory, and wheat-bearing ships bring down shining grain from Egypt, a wealth immense. In such wise is the heart of one drinking uplifted.

XIX

(28)

Οὐ βοῶν πάρεστι σώματ', οὔτε χρυσός, οὔτε πορ-
φύρεοι τάπητες, ἀλλὰ θυμὸς εὐμενής
Μοῦσά τε γλυκεῖα καὶ Βοιωτίοισιν ἐν σκύφοισιν
οἶνος ἡδύς.

Here are no bodies of oxen, nor gold, nor purple coverlets, but a kindly spirit, and the sweet muse, and mellow wine in Boeotian cups.

XX

(29)

Cassandra's Prophecy

Ὦ Τρῶες ἀρηίφιλοι, Ζεὺς ὑψιμέδων, ὃς ἅπαντα δέρ-
κεται,
οὐκ αἴτιος θνατοῖς μεγάλων ἀχέων· ἀλλ' ἐν μέσῳ
κεῖται κιχεῖν
πᾶσιν ἀνθρώποισι Δίκαν ὁσίαν, ἁγνᾶς
Εὐνομίας ἀκόλουθον καὶ πινυτᾶς Θέμιδος·
ὀλβίων παῖδές νιν εὑρόντες σύνοικον.

Trojans, beloved of Ares, it is not Zeus, ruling on high, the all-seeing, who is the cause to mortals of great sorrows. But it lies within the reach of all men to attain to holy Justice, servant of sacred Order and wise Law. Blessed are they whose children have found her their housemate.

XXI

(30)

Φάσομαι
πιστὸν κῦδος ἔχειν ἀρετάν·
πλοῦτος δὲ καὶ δειλοῖσιν ἀνθρώπων ὁμιλεῖ.

My word shall be that virtue has sure glory, but wealth consorts also with the base among men.

XXII

(33)

Hercules at the house of Ceyx

Ἔστα δ' ἐπὶ λάϊνον οὐδόν, τοὶ δὲ θοίνας ἔντυον, ὧδέ τ' ἔφα·
Αὐτόματοι δ' ἀγαθῶν δαῖτας εὐόχθους ἐπέρχονται δίκαιοι
φῶτες.

And he stood at the stone threshold, and they were preparing a banquet, and thus he spake: 'Just men come unbidden to the rich feasts of the good.'

XXIII

(34)

The Gods

Οἱ μὲν ἀδμᾶτες ἀεικελιᾶν εἰσὶ νόσων καὶ ἄνατοι,
οὐδὲν ἀνθρώποις ἴκελοι.

Unvanquished are they by ravaging diseases, and free from hurt, in no wise like men.

XXIV
(36)

Θνατοῖσι δ' οὐκ αὐθαίρετοι
οὔτ' ὄλβος οὔτ' ἄκαμπτος Ἄρης οὔτε πάμφθερσις στάσις,
ἀλλ' ἐπιχρίμπτει νέφος ἄλλοτ' ἐπ' ἄλλαν
γαῖαν ἁ πάνδωρος αἶσα.

Neither prosperity, nor unbending war, nor all-destroying faction are within mortals' choice, but destiny, that bestows all, casts a cloud now upon this land and now upon that.

XXV
(37)

Εἰ δὲ λέγει τις ἄλλως, πλατεῖα κέλευθος.

And if any one says otherwise, the path is broad.

XXVI
(38)

Μελαγκευθές εἴδωλον ἀνδρὸς Ἰθακησίου.

The black-robed shade of him of Ithaca.

XXVII
(39)

Τὰν ἀχείμαντόν τε Μέμφιν καὶ δονακώδεα Νεῖλον.

Memphis unvexed by storms and the reedy Nile.

XXVIII
(40)

Ἑκάτα δᾳδοφόρε Νυκτὸς μελανοκόλπου θύγατερ.

Hecate, torch-bearing daughter of Night the dark-bosomed.

XXIX
(41)

Ποσειδάνιον ὡς Μαντινεῖς τριόδοντα
χαλκοδαιδάλοισιν ἐν ἀσπίσι φορεῦντες.

Like the men of Mantinea who bear Poseidon's trident on their brass-wrought shields.

XXX
(44)

Ὀργαὶ μὲν ἀνθρώπων διακεκριμέναι μυρίαι.

The natures of men are diverse, myriad-numbered.

XXXI
(47)

The Eagle

Νωμᾶται δ' ἐν ἀτρυγέτῳ χάει.

And wings its way in the harvestless waste of air.

MELANIPPIDES

This poet, a native of Melos, belongs to the latter portion of the fifth century B.C., and spent a great part of his life at the court of Perdiccas II. of Macedon. He was one of the innovating school of dithyrambists, in particular removing the musical accompaniment from its former fixed laws, and allowing it to move at the composer's will. He had an extremely high reputation in his art.

I

(1)

The Danaides

Οὐ γὰρ ἀνθρώπων φόρευν μορφᾶεν εἶδος,[1]
οὐ δίαιταν τὰν γυναικείαν ἔχον,
ἀλλ' ἐν ἁρμάτεσσι διφρούχοις ἐγυμνάζοντ' ἂν εὖ,
δι' ἄλσεα πολλάκι θήραισιν φρένα τερπόμεναι,
ἠθ' ἱερόδακρυν λίβανον εὐώδεις τε φοίνικας κασίαν
  τε ματεῦσαι,
τέρενα Σύρια σπέρματα.

For they bore not the comely shape of men, yet had not the way of life of women, but in seated chariots they would take goodly toil, oft delighting their heart with hunting through the woodland, or seeking the frankincense tree that drops holy tears, and the fragrant palms and casia, tender Syrian growths.

II

(2)

Ἁ μὲν Ἀθάνα
ὄργαν' ἔρριψέν θ' ἱερᾶς ἀπὸ χειρός,
εἶπέ τ'· Ἔρρετ' αἴσχεα, σώματι λύμα,
οὔ με τᾷδ' ἐγὼ κακότατι δίδωμι.

From her sacred hand Athene cast the flute and said: 'Get thee gone, thou horror, thou out-

---

[1] Bergk prints the corrupt μορφὰν ἐνεῖδος.

rage to the body, I give not myself to this unsightliness.'

III
(4)

Πάντες δ' ἀπεστύγεον ὕδωρ,
τὸ πρὶν ἐόντες ἄϊδριες οἴνου,
τάχα δὴ τάχα τοὶ μὲν ἀπ' ὦν ὄλοντο,
τοὶ δὲ παράπληκτον χέον ὀμφάν.

And all men loathed water, for till then they had not knowledge of wine, and quickly, quickly some perished therefrom, and some gave forth a frenzy-stricken cry.

IV
(6)

Κλῦθί μοι, ὦ πάτερ, θαῦμα βροτῶν,
τᾶς ἀειζώου μεδέων ψυχᾶς.

Give ear to me, O father, wondrous in the eyes of mortals, lord of everlasting life.

ARIPHRON

The following Paean to Health is attributed to Ariphron of Sicyon, of whom nothing further is known. The fact of its being addressed to an abstract deity shows that it belongs to a late period of lyric poetry.

Ὑγίεια, πρεσβίστα μακάρων, μετὰ σεῦ ναίοιμι τὸ
  λειπόμενον
βιοτᾶς, σὺ δέ μοι πρόφρων σύνοικος εἴης·
εἰ γάρ τις ἢ πλούτου χάρις ἢ τεκέων,
ἢ τᾶς ἰσοδαίμονος ἀνθρώποις βασιληΐδος ἀρχᾶς, ἢ
  πόθων,
οὓς κρυφίοις Ἀφροδίτας ἕρκεσιν θηρεύομεν,
ἢ εἴ τις ἄλλα θεόθεν ἀνθρώποισι τέρψις ἢ πόνων
  ἀμπνοὰ πέφανται,
μετὰ σεῖο, μάκαιρ' Ὑγίεια,
τέθαλε [πάντα] καὶ λάμπει Χαρίτων ἔαρι,
σέθεν δὲ χωρὶς οὔτις εὐδαίμων (ἔφυ).

Health, most honoured of deities, may I dwell with thee for what remains of life, and mayest thou be my willing housemate! For whatever joy of wealth, or children, or of kingly power that makes men equal with the gods, or of love that we hunt with the hidden snares of Aphrodite, or whatever other delight or rest from toils has appeared to men from on high, has goodly growth and is radiant with the bloom of the graces, when joined with thee, divine Health; but apart from thee no man is happy.

LICYMNIUS

A dithyrambic poet of Chios of uncertain date.

I
(1)
Acheron

Μυρίαις παγαῖς δακρύων ἀχέων τε βρύει.

With founts numberless of tears and sorrows it is full.

II
(3)
Endymion

Ὕπνος δὲ χαίρων ὀμμάτων αὐγαῖς ἀναπεπταμένοις
ὄσσοις ἐκοίμιζε κοῦρον.

And Sleep, taking joy in the brightness of his gaze, laid the boy to rest with open eyes.

III
(4)

Λιπαρόμματε μᾶτερ, ὑψίστων θρόνων
σεμνῶν Ἀπόλλωνος βασίλεια ποθεινά,
πραϋγέλως Ὑγίεια.

Bright-eyed mother, fair queen of Apollo's highest, holy seats, soft-laughing Health.

PHILOXENUS

Philoxenus of Cythera (435-380 B.C.) was a pupil of Melanippides, and introduced still further changes into dithyrambic composition. He lived at Athens, and afterwards under the protection of Dionysius the elder at Syracuse. The following fragments are from his Cyclops. The second is the address of the Cyclops to Galatea, the third the exclamation of Ulysses in the Cyclops' cave, and the fourth is addressed by the Cyclops to Ulysses in reference to the slaughter of his sheep. Considerable fragments remain of what was the most popular of his poems, one giving a minute account of a banquet, but it is impossible to regard it as possessing the characteristics of the lyric.

I

(6)

Συμβαλοῦμαί τι μέλος ὑμῖν εἰς ἔρωτα.

A song that tells of love will I impart to you.

II

(8)

Ὦ καλλιπρόσωπε
χρυσοβόστρυχε Γαλάτεια
χαριτόφωνε, θάλος ἐρώτων.

O fair-faced Galatea of the golden tresses, gracious in voice, nursling of the loves.

III

(9)

Οἵῳ μ' ὁ δαίμων τέρατι συγκαθεῖρξεν.

With what a monster has fate shut me in.

IV

(10)

Ἔθυσας; ἀντιθύσῃ.

Hast sacrificed? Thou shalt in turn be sacrificed.

TIMOTHEUS

Timotheus of Miletus (454-357 B.C.) was one of the chief representatives of the dithyrambic innovators (*cf.* Frag. VII.), and enjoyed enormous popularity, both during his lifetime and long afterwards.

I

(5)

Ἔχευε δ' ἐν μὲν δέπας κίσσινον μελαίνας
σταγόνος ἀμβρότας ἀφρῷ βρυάζον·
εἴκοσιν δὲ μέτρ' ἀνέχευεν ἔμισγέ θ'
αἷμα Βακχίου νεορρύτοις δακρύοισι Νυμφᾶν.

And he poured out one cup of ivy-wood, brimming with the foam of the dark juice divine, and with it twenty measures of water, mingling the blood of Bacchus with the fresh-flowing tears of the Nymphs.

(6)

Quoted by Zeno the Stoic in reference to the death which he inflicted upon himself after receiving an injury from a fall.

Ἔρχομαι· τί μ' αὔεις;

I am coming, why callest thou me?

III

(8)

Κλεινὸν ἐλευθερίας τεύχων μέγαν Ἑλλάδι κόσμον.

Working for Hellas the great glorious honour of freedom.

IV

(9)

Σέβεσθ' αἰδῶ σύνεργον ἀρετᾶς δοριμάχου.

Have reverence for honour, the helpmate of valour fighting with the spear.

V

(10)

Ἄρης τύραννος· χρυσὸν Ἑλλὰς δ' οὐ δέδοικεν.

Ares is lord, but gold Hellas does not fear.

VI

(11)

Μακάριος ἦσθα, Τιμόθεε, κᾶρυξ ὅτ' εἶπεν·
νικᾷ Τιμόθεος Μιλήσιος
τὸν Κάμωνος τὸν ἰωνοκάμπταν.

Happy thou wert, Timotheus, when the herald said: Timotheus of Miletus vanquishes the son of Camon, the triller of Ionian flourishes.

VII

(12)

Οὐκ ἀείδω τὰ παλαιά,
καινὰ γὰρ μάλα κρείσσω·
νέος ὁ Ζεὺς βασιλεύει,
τὸ πάλαι δ' ἦν Κρόνος ἄρχων·
ἀπίτω Μοῦσα παλαιά.

I sing not ancient strains, for the later are far goodlier. Zeus is the new king, but of old Cronos was ruler; let the Muse of old times depart.

VIII

(13)

Σύ τ' ὦ τὸν ἀεὶ πόλον οὐράνιον
ἀκτῖσι λαμπραῖς Ἅλιε βάλλων,
πέμψον ἑκαβόλον ἐχθροῖς βέλος
σᾶς ἀπὸ νευρᾶς, ὦ ἰὲ Παιάν.

And do thou, O Sun, ever smiting with bright beams the vault of heaven, send from thy bow-string a far-cast dart upon our foes, O Paean!

IX

(14)

Σὺ δὲ τὸν γηγενέταν ἄργυρον αἰνεῖς.

But you praise earth-born silver.

The words were addressed as a reproach to the Macedonian king Archelaus, who retorted with σὺ δέ γ' αἰτεῖς, 'and you ask for it.'

x

(15)

Οὔθ' ὁ πτερωτὸς ἰξὸς ὀμμάτων, Ἔρως,
ὁ Κύπριδος κυναγός, ἡ φρενῶν ἄκις,
ὁ μὴ τίνων θεοῖσιν ὁρκίων δίκας.

Nor Love, the winged lure of the eyes, Aphrodite's huntsman, the barb of the soul, who makes not atonement to the gods for broken oaths.

TELESTES

A native of Selinus in Sicily, who flourished as a dithyrambic poet at Athens about 400 B.C.

1

(1)

Ὃν σοφὸν σοφὰν λαβοῦσαν οὐκ ἐπέλπομαι νόῳ
  δρυμοῖς ὀρείοις
ὀργάνων δίαν Ἀθάναν
δυσόφθαλμον αἶσχος ἐκφοβηθεῖσαν,
αὖθις ἐκ χερῶν βαλεῖν,
νυμφαγενεῖ χοροκτύπῳ φηρὶ Μαρσύᾳ κλέος.
τί γάρ νιν εὐηράτοιο κάλλεος ὀξὺς ἔρως ἔτειρεν,
ᾇ παρθενίαν ἄγαμον καὶ ἄπαιδ' ἀπένειμε Κλωθώ;
ἀλλὰ μάταν ἀχόρευτος
ἅδε ματαιολόγων φάμα προσέπταθ' Ἑλλάδα μουσο-
  πόλων,
σοφᾶς ἐπίφθονον βροτοῖς τέχνας ὄνειδος,
τὰν . . .[1] Βρομίῳ παρέδωκε σεμνᾶς
δαίμονος ἀερθὲν πνεῦμα λιγυπτέρυγον σὺν ἀγλαᾶν
  ὠκύτατι χειρῶν.

And this instrument, wisely devised, I deem not in my mind that the wise goddess Athene, for fear of the eye-grieving unsightliness wrought by the flute, having taken it up in the mountain glades, cast again from her hands,—a triumph to the

[1] Bergk here prints the corrupt οὐ μεριθοτάταν.

nymph-born, dance-treading satyr Marsyas. For why did keen desire for lovely fairness consume her to whom Fate assigned unwedded and childless maidenhood? Nay, this doleful story of idly-prating minstrels sped falsely over Hellas, an envious reproach in the ears of mortals of the wise art which the uplifted, shrill-winged breath of the holy goddess, and the swift movement of her goodly hands, gave to the service of Bromius.

II

(2)

Ἡ Φρύγα καλλιπνόων αὐλῶν ἱερῶν βασιλῆα,
Λυδὸν ὃς ἅρμοσε πρῶτος
Δωρίδος ἀντίπαλον μούσας νόμον αἰόλον ὀμφᾷ,
πνεύματος εὔπτερον αὔραν ἀμφιπλέκων καλάμοις.

Or the Phrygian lord of holy, sweet-breathing flutes, who first fitted to the voice the changeful Lydian mode, rival of the Dorian strain, entangling in reeds the winged current of the breath.

III

(4)

Ἄλλος δ᾽ ἄλλαν κλαγγὰν ἱείς
κερατόφωνον ἠρέθιζε μάγαδιν,
ἐν πενταράβῳ χορδᾶν ἀρθμῷ
χεῖρα καμψιδίαυλον ἀναστρωφῶν τάχος.

And one giving forth one sound, one another, they roused the harp with its echoing board of horn, swiftly running the hand to and fro along the five-staved sequence of the chords.

IV

(5)

Πρῶτοι παρὰ κρατῆρας Ἑλλάνων ἐν αὐλοῖς
συνοπαδοὶ Πέλοπος ματρὸς ὀρείας
Φρύγιον ἄεισαν νόμον·
τοὶ δ' ὀξυφώνοις πηκτίδων ψαλμοῖς κρέκον
Λύδιον ὕμνον.

Over the wine-bowls of the Greeks the companions of Pelops were the first to sing to the sound of flutes the Phrygian harmony of the mountain mother, and some with the sharp twang of harp-strings beat out the Lydian strain.

LYCOPHRONIDES

A dithyrambic poet of uncertain date.

I
(1)

Οὔτε παιδὸς ἄρρενος οὔτε παρθένων
τῶν χρυσοφόρων οἴτε γυναικῶν βαθυκόλπων
καλὸν τὸ πρόσωπον, ἂν μὴ κόσμιον πεφύκῃ.
ἡ γὰρ αἰδὼς ἄνθος ἐπισπείρει.

No face of youth, or gold-decked maidens, or deep-girdled women is fair, if it be not seemly; for modesty sheddeth grace.

II
(2)

Τόδ' ἀνατίθημί σοι ῥόδον
καλὸν ἀνάθημα καὶ πέδιλα καὶ κυνέαν
καὶ τὰν θηροφόνον λογχίδ', ἐπεί μοι νόος ἄλλᾳ
κέχυται
ἐπὶ τὰν Χάρισιν φίλαν πάιδα καὶ καλάν.

This rose I offer up to thee, a goodly offering, and my sandals and cap and beast-slaying spear, since my mind has set elsewhither towards a maiden loved of the Graces, and beauteous.

CASTORIO

A native of Soli in Cilicia, who lived during the end of the fourth and beginning of the third century B.C.

I

(2)

Σὲ τὸν βολαῖς νιφοκτύποις δυσχείμερον
ναίονθ' ἕδραν, θηρονόμε Πάν, χθόν' Ἀρκάδων,
κλήσω γραφῇ τῇδ' ἐν σοφῇ πάγκλειτ' ἔπη
συνθείς, ἄναξ, δύσγνωστα μὴ σοφῷ κλύειν,
μωσοπόλε θήρ, κηρόχυτον ὃς μείλιγμ' ἵεις.

Thee, beast-tending Pan, dwelling in the land of the Arcadians, in haunts wintry with loud snowblasts, thee I will celebrate, fitting together, O king, in this wise lay words right glorious, hard for the unwise to hear with understanding, O minstrel satyr, that breathest a soft strain through the wax-moulded pipe.

SCOLIA OR BANQUET-SONGS

It is uncertain in what sense the word σκολιόν, 'crooked,' was applied to a banquet-song. The usual explanation is that it refers to the irregular order in which the song was taken up by the guests.

SCOLIA

I
(1)

Οὐδὲν ἦν ἄρα τἄλλα πλὴν ὁ χρυσός.

So, then, all things are naught, except gold.

II
(2)

Παλλὰς Τριτογένει᾽, ἄνασσ᾽ Ἀθηνᾶ,
ὄρθου τήνδε πόλιν τε καὶ πολίτας
ἄτερ ἀλγέων καὶ στάσεων
καὶ θανάτων ἀώρων σύ τε καὶ πατήρ.

Triton-born Pallas, queen Athene, maintain this city and its citizens without griefs and factions and untimely deaths, thou and thy sire.

III
(3)

Πλούτου μητέρ᾽, Ὀλυμπίαν ἀείδω
Δήμητρα στεφανηφόροις ἐν ὥραις,
σέ τε παῖ Διὸς Φερσεφόνη·
χαίρετον, εὖ δὲ τάνδ᾽ ἀμφέπετον πόλιν.

I sing in the garland-wearing hour of Olympian Demeter, mother of wealth, and of thee, Persephone, daughter of Zeus. Hail to ye, and do ye guard well this city.

IV

(4)

Ἐν Δήλῳ ποτ' ἔτικτε τέκνα Λατώ,
Φοῖβον χρυσοκόμαν, ἄνακτ' Ἀπόλλω,
ἐλαφηβόλον τ' ἀγροτέραν
Ἄρτεμιν, ἃ γυναικῶν μέγ' ἔχει κράτος.

In Delos once upon a time Leto bare children, golden-haired Phoebus, king Apollo, and huntress Artemis, slayer of stags, who has great dominion over women.

V

(5)

Ὦ Πάν, Ἀρκαδίας μεδέων κλεεννᾶς,
ὀρχηστά, Βρομίαις ὀπαδὲ Νύμφαις,
γελάσειας, ὦ Πάν, ἐπ' ἐμαῖς
εὐφροσύναισι, ταῖσδ' ἀοιδαῖς κεχαρημένος.

Pan, lord of famed Arcady, Pan the dancer, companion of the nymphs of Bacchus, mayest thou smile upon my mirth, taking joy in these strains.

VI

(7)

Εἴθ' ἐξῆν ὁποῖός τις ἦν ἕκαστος
τὸ στῆθος διελόντ', ἔπειτα τὸν νοῦν
ἐσιδόντα, κλείσαντα πάλιν,
ἄνδρα φίλον νομίζειν ἀδόλῳ φρενί.

Would that it were possible, having opened the breast, to then behold the soul, so as to learn of what nature a man was, and having closed it again to know him for a friend with guileless heart.

VII
(8)

Ὑγιαίνειν μὲν ἄριστον ἀνδρὶ θνατῷ,
δεύτερον δὲ φυὰν καλὸν γενέσθαι,
τὸ τρίτον δὲ πλουτεῖν ἀδόλως,
καὶ τὸ τέταρτον ἡβᾶν μετὰ τῶν φίλων.

The best thing for a mortal is to have health, and the next to have been born fair of form, and the third to be rich without guile, and the fourth to take joy with one's friends.

VIII
(9-12)

Ἐν μύρτου κλαδὶ τὸ ξίφος φορήσω,
ὥσπερ Ἁρμόδιος καὶ Ἀριστογείτων,
ὅτε τὸν τύραννον κτανέτην
ἰσονόμους τ' Ἀθήνας ἐποιησάτην.

Φίλταθ' Ἁρμόδι', οὔ τί που τέθνηκας,
νήσοις δ' ἐν μακάρων σέ φασιν εἶναι,
ἵνα περ ποδώκης Ἀχιλεύς,
Τυδείδην τέ φασιν ἐσθλὸν Διομήδεα.

Ἐν μύρτου κλαδὶ τὸ ξίφος φορήσω,
ὥσπερ Ἁρμόδιος καὶ Ἀριστογείτων,
ὅτ' Ἀθηναίης ἐν θυσίαις
ἄνδρα τύραννον Ἵππαρχον ἐκαινέτην.

Αἰεὶ σφῷν κλέος ἔσσεται κατ' αἶαν,
φίλταθ' Ἁρμόδιος καὶ Ἀριστογείτων,
ὅτι τὸν τύραννον κτάνετον,[1]
ἰσονόμους τ' Ἀθήνας ἐποιήσατον.

In a bough of myrtle will I bear my sword, even as Harmodius and Aristogeiton when they slew the tyrant, and made Athens to have equal laws.

Dearest Harmodius, surely thou art not dead, but men say that thou art in the islands of the blest, where swift-footed Achilles is, and where, they say, is glorious Diomed, the son of Tydeus.

In a bough of myrtle will I bear my sword, even as Harmodius and Aristogeiton when they slew the tyrant Hipparchus at Athene's festival.

For ever shall your fame, dearest Harmodius and Aristogeiton, endure in the land, because ye slew the tyrant, and made Athens to have equal laws.

IX
(14)

The reference is to the defeat of the Athenian exiles by Hippias.

Αἰαῖ Λειψύδριον προδωσέταιρον,
οἵους ἄνδρας ἀπώλεσας, μάχεσθαι
ἀγαθούς τε χἄμ' εὐπατρίδας,
οἳ τότ' ἔδειξαν οἵων πατέρων ἔσαν.

Alas, Leipsydrium, betrayer of comrades, what men didst thou destroy, good at the fight and

---

[1] Bergk κτανέτην, and in the next line ἐποιησάτην.

withal of noble race, who then did show from what sires they were sprung.

X
(15)

Ἐκ γῆς χρὴ κατιδεῖν πλόον,
εἴ τις δύναιτο καὶ παλάμην ἔχοι·
ἐπεὶ δέ κ' ἐν πόντῳ γένηται,
τῷ παρεόντι τρέχειν ἀνάγκη.

A man should consider a voyage from the land, to see if he would be able and would have the skill; but when he has come upon the deep, he must needs run with the wind there is.

XI
(16)

Ὁ καρκίνος ὧδ' ἔφα
χαλᾷ τὸν ὄφιν λαβών·
εὐθὺν χρὴ τὸν ἑταῖρον ἔμμεν
καὶ μὴ σκολιὰ φρονεῖν.

The crab spake these words, seizing the snake with his claw: 'A comrade should be straight and not think crookedly.'

XII
(19)

Εἴθε λύρα καλὴ γενοίμην ἐλεφαντίνη,
καί με καλοὶ παῖδες φέροιεν Διονύσιον ἐς χορόν.

Would that I might be a fair lyre of ivory, and that fair boys might carry me to the dance of Dionysus.

XIII
(20)

Εἴθ' ἄπυρον καλὸν γενοίμην μέγα χρυσίον,
καί με καλὴ γυνὴ φοροίη καθαρὸν θεμένη νόον.

Would that I might be a golden jewel, fair and great, needing not to be refined by fire, and that a fair woman might bear me, having made pure her heart.

XIV
(22)

Σύν μοι πῖνε, συνήβα, συνέρα, στεφανηφόρει,
σύν μοι μαινομένῳ μαίνεο, σὺν σώφρονι σωφρόνει.

Drink with me, take joy with me, love with me, wear garlands with me, be mad with me in my madness, and sober in my soberness.

XV
(23)

Ὑπὸ παντὶ λίθῳ σκορπίος, ὦ 'ταῖρ', ὑποδύεται·
φράζευ, μή σε βάλῃ· τῷ δ' ἀφανεῖ πᾶς ἕπεται δόλος.

Under every stone, O friend, there lurks a scorpion; beware lest it sting thee: all guile doth attend the hidden.

XVI
(28)

The song of Hybrias, a Cretan noble.

Ἔστι μοι πλοῦτος μέγας δόρυ καὶ ξίφος
καὶ τὸ καλὸν λαισήϊον, πρόβλημα χρωτός·

τούτῳ γὰρ ἀρῶ, τούτῳ θερίζω,
τούτῳ πατέω τὸν ἁδὺν οἶνον ἀπ' ἀμπέλω·
τούτῳ δεσπότας μνοίας κέκλημαι.

Τοὶ δὲ μὴ τολμῶντ' ἔχειν δόρυ καὶ ξίφος
καὶ τὸ καλὸν λαισήϊον, πρόβλημα χρωτός·
πάντες γόνυ πεπτηῶτες (ἀμφὶ)
ἐμόν . . . (προσ)κυνεῦντί (με) δεσπόταν
καὶ μέγαν βασιλῆα φωνέοντες.

In my spear and sword I have plenteous wealth, and in the goodly shield that screens the body, for with these I plough, I reap, I tread the sweet wine from the grape, through these I am named the lord of serfs.

But those who fear to bear spear and sword, and the goodly shield that screens the body, all they, crouching round my knee, do homage to me as lord, calling me great king.

XVII
(30)

Οὐ χρὴ πόλλ' ἔχειν θνητὸν ἄνθρωπον, ἀλλ' ἐρᾶν,
καὶ κατεσθίειν· σὺ δὲ κάρτα φείδῃ.

It needs not for a mortal to have many possessions, but that he should love and feast; but in thee there is great abstinence.

CARMINA POPULARIA

The following specimens of popular poetry deal mainly with religious ritual, and children's games and songs. The concluding passage, however, has reference to a definite historical occasion, and is not very appropriately classed by Bergk under this head.

I

(1)

To Demeter

Πλεῖστον οὖλον ἵει, ἴουλον ἵει.

Many a sheaf, many a sheaf do thou send forth.

II

(2)

Ὦ Λίνε (πᾶσι) θεοῖσιν
τετιμένε, σοὶ γὰρ ἔδωκαν
πρώτῳ μέλος ἀνθρώποισιν
φωναῖς λιγυραῖς ἀεῖσαι·
Φοῖβος δὲ κότῳ σ' ἀναιρεῖ,
Μοῦσαι δέ σε θρηνεύουσιν.

O Linus, honoured by all the gods, for to thee they granted that thou shouldst first give forth song to mortals in clear notes:—but Phoebus from envy killed thee, and the Muses mourn for thee.

III

(4)

Ἀνάβαλ' ἄνω τὸ γῆρας,
ὦ καλὰ Ἀφροδίτα.

Keep old age far off, O beauteous Aphrodite.

IV

(6)

Ἐλθεῖν, ἥρω Διόνυσε,
Ἀλείων ἐς ναόν
ἁγνὸν σὺν Χαρίτεσσιν,
ἐς ναόν
τῷ βοέῳ ποδὶ θύων.
ἄξιε ταῦρε,
ἄξιε ταῦρε.

Come, hero Dionysus, with the Graces to the holy temple of the Eleans, speeding with ox's foot to the temple, O glorious, glorious bull!

V

(8)

Σοί, Βάκχε, τάνδε μοῦσαν ἀγλαΐζομεν
ἁπλοῦν ῥυθμὸν χέοντες αἰόλῳ μέλει,
καίναν, ἀπαρθένευτον, οὔτι ταῖς πάρος
κεχρημέναν ᾠδαῖσιν, ἀλλ' ἀκήρατον
κατάρχομεν τὸν ὕμνον.

Thee, Bacchus, we honour with this strain, pouring forth one measure in varying melody, a strain that is new, unmeet for maidens, taking nought from older lays, but unstaled by use is the chant that we begin.

VI
(11)

Τίς τῇδε; πολλοὶ κἀγαθοί.
Ἐκκέχυται· κάλει θεόν.

Who is here? Many men and good.
Libation has been made; call thou upon the god.

VII
(12)

Ἥλιος Ἀπόλλων, ὁ δέ γ' Ἀπόλλων ἥλιος.

The sun is Apollo, and Apollo is the sun.

VIII
(14)

Ἄρχει μὲν ἀγὼν τῶν καλλίστων
ἄθλων ταμίας, καιρὸς δὲ καλεῖ
μηκέτι μέλλειν.

The contest begins, making award of prizes most glorious, and the hour calls to no longer delay.

IX
(15)

Βαλβῖδι ποδῶν
θέντες πόδα πὰρ πόδα (θεῖτε).

Place foot by foot at the starting-line of the feet, and run!

X

(16)

Λήγει μὲν ἀγὼν τῶν καλλίστων
ἄθλων ταμίας, καιρὸς δὲ καλεῖ
μηκέτι μέλλειν.

The contest ends, making award of prizes most glorious, and the hour calls to no longer delay.

XI

(18)

Sung by the Spartan choruses of old men, men, and boys.

'Ἀμὲς πόκ' ἦμες ἄλκιμοι νεανίαι.
'Ἀμὲς δέ γ' εἰμές· αἰ δὲ λῇς, αὐγάσδεο.
'Ἀμὲς δέ γ' ἐσσόμεσθα πολλῷ κάρρονες.

We were once valiant young men.
And we are so, and, if you will, look upon us.
And we shall be far better.

XII

(19)

Ποῦ μοι τὰ ῥόδα, ποῦ μοι τὰ ἴα, ποῦ μοι τὰ καλὰ σέλινα;
Ταδὶ τὰ ῥόδα, ταδὶ τὰ ἴα, ταδὶ τὰ καλὰ σέλινα.

Where are my roses, where are my violets, where is my pretty parsley?
Here are the roses, here are the violets, here is the pretty parsley.

XIII

(20)

Blind Man's Buff

Χαλκῆν μυῖαν θηράσω.
Θηράσεις, ἀλλ' οὐ λήψει.

I will hunt a brazen fly.
You will hunt, but you will not catch.

XIV

(21)

Χέλει χελώνη, τί ποιεῖς ἐν τῷ μέσῳ;
Μαρύομ' ἔρια καὶ κρόκαν Μιλησίαν.
Ὁ δ' ἔκγονός σου τί ποιῶν ἀπώλετο;
Λευκᾶν ἀφ' ἵππων εἰς θάλασσαν ἅλατο.

Tortoise, tortoise, what are you doing in the midst?
I am weaving wool and Milesian thread.
And how came your son to perish?
He leapt from white horses into the sea.

XV

(22 A)

Ἔξεχ', ὦ φίλ' Ἥλιε.

Shine out, dear sun.

XVI
(26)

Στρίγγ' ἀποπομπεῖν
νυκτιβόαν (γᾶς),
στρίγγ' ἀπὸ λαῶν,
ὄρνιν ἀνώνυμον (ἐχθρῶν)
ὠκυπόρους ἐπὶ νῆας.

Send the night-crying owl, bird of evil name, away from the land and peoples, to the swift-voyaging ships of our foes.

XVII
(27)

Ὦ τί πάσχεις; μὴ προδῷς ἄμμ', ἱκετεύω·
πρὶν καὶ μολὲν κεῖνον, ἀνίστω·
μὴ κακὸν σὲ μέγα ποιήσῃς κἠμὲ τὰν δειλάκραν·
ἀμέρα καὶ δή· τὸ φῶς ζὰ τῆς θυρίδος οὐκ ὀρῇς;

Ah, what has come to thee? Betray me not, I entreat thee. Before that he comes, arise, and bring not great evil upon thyself and me the unhappy. Already it is day; seest thou not the light through the window?

XVIII
(41)

Song of the Rhodian Children

Ἦλθ', ἦλθε χελιδών,
καλὰς ὥρας ἄγουσα,
καλοὺς ἐνιαυτούς,

ἐπὶ γαστέρα λευκά,
ἐπὶ νῶτα μέλαινα.
παλάθαν σὺ προκύκλει
ἐκ πίονος οἴκου,
οἴνου τε δέπαστρον,
τυρῶν τε κάννυστρον·
καὶ πύρνα χελιδών
καὶ λεκιθίταν
οὐκ ἀπωθεῖται. πότερ᾽ ἀπίωμες, ἢ λαβώμεθα;
εἰ μέν τι δώσεις· εἰ δὲ μή, οὐκ ἐάσομεν,
ἢ τὰν θύραν φέρωμες ἢ τοὐπέρθυρον,
ἢ τὰν γυναῖκα τὰν ἔσω καθημέναν·
μικρὰ μέν ἐστι, ῥᾳδίως μιν οἴσομεν.
ἂν δὲ φέρῃς τι,
μέγα δή τι φέροιο.
ἄνοιγ᾽, ἄνοιγε τὰν θύραν χελιδόνι·
οὐ γὰρ γέροντές ἐσμεν, ἀλλὰ παιδία.

The swallow, the swallow has come, bringing fair hours and fair seasons, white upon its belly, black upon its back. Roll forth a cake from the rich house, and a flagon of wine, and a basket of cheese; wheaten bread, too, and bread of pulse the swallow refuses not. Are we to depart or to receive? If you give us something, rest you so; but if you say us nay, we will not suffer it. Let us bear away the door or the lintel, or the wife sitting within; she is little, we will bear her away easily. But if you bring us something, may your own gain be great. Open, open the door to the swallow, for we are not old men, but children.

XIX
(43)

Ἄλει μύλα ἄλει·
καὶ γὰρ Πιττακὸς ἄλει,
μεγάλας Μιτυλάνας βασιλεύων.

Grind, mill, grind, for Pittacus also ground, ruling over great Mitylene.

XX
(44)

Ὦ παῖδες, ὅσοι Χαρίτων τε καὶ πατέρων λάχετ
  ἐσθλῶν,
μὴ φθονεῖθ᾽ ὥρας ἀγαθοῖσιν ὁμιλίαν·
σὺν γὰρ ἀνδρείᾳ καὶ ὁ λυσιμελὴς ἔρως ἐπὶ Χαλκιδέωι
  θάλλει πόλεσιν.

O all ye youths that have won the favour of the Graces and noble ancestry, grudge not communion with your fairness to the honourable; for love, that makes loose the limbs, blooms side by side with valour in the cities of the Chalcidians.

XXI
(46)

Hymn addressed by the Athenians to Demetrius Poliorcetes, 302 B.C.

Ὥς[1] οἱ μέγιστοι τῶν θεῶν καὶ φίλτατοι
τῇ πόλει πάρεισιν·
ἐνταῦθα (γὰρ Δήμητρα καὶ) Δημήτριον
ἅμα παρῆγ᾽ ὁ καιρός.

[1] Bergk, Ὥς.

χἢ μὲν τὰ σεμνὰ τῆς Κόρης μυστήρια
ἔρχεθ', ἵνα ποιήσῃ,
ὁ δ' ἱλαρός, ὥσπερ τὸν θεὸν δεῖ, καὶ καλός
καὶ γελῶν πάρεστιν.
σεμνόν τι φαίνεθ', οἱ φίλοι πάντες κύκλῳ,
ἐν μέσοισι δ' αὐτός·
ὅμοιον, ὥσπερ οἱ φίλοι μὲν ἀστέρες,
ἥλιος δ' ἐκεῖνος.
ὦ τοῦ κρατίστου παῖ Ποσειδῶνος θεοῦ
χαῖρε κἀφροδίτης·
ἄλλοι μὲν ἢ μακρὰν γὰρ ἀπέχουσιν θεοί,
ἢ οὐκ ἔχουσιν ὦτα,
ἢ οὐκ εἰσίν, ἢ οὐ προσέχουσιν ἡμῖν οὐδὲ ἕν,
σὲ δὲ παρόνθ' ὁρῶμεν,
οὐ ξύλινον, οὐδὲ λίθινον, ἀλλ' ἀληθινόν·
εὐχόμεσθα δή σοι.
πρῶτον μὲν εἰρήνην ποίησον, φίλτατε·
κύριος γὰρ εἶ σύ.
τὴν δ' οὐχὶ Θηβῶν, ἀλλ' ὅλης τῆς Ἑλλάδος
Σφίγγα περικρατοῦσαν,
Αἰτωλὸς ὅστις ἐπὶ πέτρας καθήμενος,
ὥσπερ ἡ παλαιά,
τὰ σώμαθ' ἡμῶν πάντ' ἀναρπάσας φέρει,
κοὐκ ἔχω μάχεσθαι·
Αἰτωλικὸν γὰρ ἁρπάσαι τὰ τῶν πέλας,
νῦν δὲ καὶ τὰ πόρρω·
μάλιστα μὲν δὴ κόλασον αὐτός· εἰ δὲ μή,
Οἰδίπουν τιν' εὑρέ,
τὴν Σφίγγα ταύτην ὅστις ἢ κατακρημνιεῖ,
ἢ σπίλον ποιήσει.

How are the greatest and best loved of deities, present at our city! for here has occasion brought at the same time Demeter and Demetrius. And she comes that she may celebrate the Daughter's solemn mysteries, but he is here joyous, as becomes a god, and comely, and laughing. 'Tis a stately show, all his friends around him, and he himself in their midst, like as though his friends were the stars, and he the sun. Child of the most mighty god Poseidon and of Aphrodite, hail to thee! for other gods are either far distant, or have not ears, or are not, or pay no manner of heed to us, but thee we see present, not graven in wood or stone, but real. We make our prayers to thee. First, O best beloved, make there to be peace, for thou art able. And the Sphinx that holds dominion not over Thebes alone, but over all Hellas, the Aetolian who seated, like the Sphinx of old, upon a rock, seizes and bears us all away, nor have I the strength to do battle,— for it is the way of the Aetolians to plunder that which is near, and now also that which is afar— do thou, best of all, bring punishment upon it thyself, or, if not that, find some Oedipus who shall either hurl this Sphinx headlong, or turn it to stone.

FRAGMENTA ADESPOTA

Under this head are included fragments of unknown authorship.

I

(20 A)

Πολλὰ δ' ἐν μεταιχμίῳ
Νότος κυλίνδει κύματ' εὐρείης ἁλός.

And the south wind rolls many waves of the broad sea between.

II

(20 B)

Οὐκ ἀξιῶ μικκῶν σε· μεγάλα δ' οὐκ ἔχω.

I deem thee not worthy of little things, and great ones I have not.

III

(23)

Δῆμος ἄστατον κακόν
καὶ θαλάσσῃ πάνθ' ὁμοῖον ὑπ' ἀνέμου ῥιπίζεται,
καὶ γαληνὸς ἢν τύχῃ, πρὸς πνεῦμα βραχὺ κορύσσεται,
κἢν τις αἰτία γένηται, τὸν πολίτην κατέπιεν.

The multitude is a fickle pest, and is ruffled by the wind just like the sea, and if it chance to be calm, it becomes crested at a light breeze, and if any offence come, it devours the offender.

IV
(53)

'Εγώ φαμι ιοπλοκάμων Μοισᾶν εὖ λαχεῖν.

I say that I have won grace of the violet-haired Muses.

V
(62)

'Εκ Σάπφως τόδ' ἀμελγόμενος μέλι τοι φέρω.

From Sappho I press and bring to thee this honey.

VI
(81)

Μέλεα μελιπτέρωτα Μῶσαν.

The honey-winged songs of the Muses.

VII
(86 A)

(Μηδὲ) πᾶν ὅττι κ' ἐπ' ἀκαιρίμαν
γλῶσσαν ἔπος ἔλθῃ κελαδεῖν.

Nor speak aloud every word that may come to the untimely tongue.

VIII
(86 B)

Οὐ γὰρ ἐν μέσοισι κεῖται δῶρα δυσμάχητα Μοισᾶν
τὠπιτυχόντι φέρειν.

For the gifts of the Muses, hard to contend for, lie not in the midst for the chance-comer to bear away.

IX
(87)

Ναὶ τὰν Ὄλυμπον καταδερκομέναν σκαπτοῦχον
   Ἥραν,
ἔστι μοι πιστὸν ταμιεῖον ἐπὶ γλώσσας.

By sceptre-bearing Hera, that looks down upon Olympus, I have a trusty ward-chamber upon my tongue.

X
(89)

Ὦ γλυκεῖ' εἰράνα,
πλουτοδότειρα βροτοῖς.

O sweet peace, giver of wealth to mortals.

XI
(91)

Ὅτε Τυνδαριδᾶν ἀδελφῶν ἅλιον ναύταν πόθος βάλλει.

When desire for the twin sons of Tyndareus comes upon the sailor on the deep.

XII
(92)

Hades

Νυκτὸς αἰδνᾶς ἀεργηλοῖό θ' ὕπνου κοίρανον.

Lord of hidden night and untoiling sleep.

XIII

(93)

Εὐρύοπα κέλαδον ἀκροσόφων ἀγνύμενον διὰ στομάτων.

A far-sounding cry breaking through lips high-skilled.

XIV

(94)

Οὐ ψάμμος ἢ κόνις ἢ πτερὰ ποικιλοθρόων οἰωνῶν
τόσσον ἂν χεύαιτ' ἀριθμόν.

Not sand or dust or the feathers of diverse-crying birds would yield such numbers.

XV

(96)

Ἔπειτα κείσεται βαθυδένδρῳ
ἐν χθονὶ συμποσίων τε καὶ λυρᾶν ἄμοιρος
ἰαχᾶς τε παντερπέος αὐλῶν.

Then shall he lie in the deep-wooded earth, without share in carousals and the lyre and the all-gladdening sound of flutes.

XVI

(97)

Ὣς ἄρ' εἰπόντα μιν ἀμβρόσιον
τηλαυγὲς ἐλασίππου πρόσωπον
ἀπέλιπεν ἀμέρας.

When he had thus spoken, the divine, far-shining face of steed-drawn day passed from him.

XVII
(98)

Οὐκ αἰεὶ θαλέθοντι βίῳ
βλάσταις τε τέκνων βριθομένα γλυκερόν
φάος ὁρῶσα.

Beholding the sweet light not with her life ever prosperous, nor richly laden with the fruit of offspring.

XVIII
(99)

"Αλλον τρόπον ἄλλον ἐγείρει
φροντὶς ἀνθρώπων.

One man in one way, one in another care doth harass.

XIX
(101)

Hecuba

. . . χαροπὰν κύνα· χάλκεον δέ οἱ
γναθμῶν ἐκ πολιᾶν φθεγγομένας ὑπάκουε μὲν Ἴδα.
Τένεδός τε περίρρυτα
Ὀρηἴκιοί τε (πάγοι) φιλάνεμοί τε πέτραι.

(The Furies made her) a dog with flaming eyes, and Ida and sea-girt Tenedos, and the hills and wind-loving rocks of Thrace hearkened to her uttering a brazen cry from hoary jaws.

XX
(104 A)

Ποικίλλεται μὲν γαῖα πολυστέφανος.

Variously adorned is the earth, many-garlanded.

XXI
(104 B)

Οὐ μήποτε τὰν ἀρετὰν ἀλλάξομαι ἀντ' ἀδίκου κέρδους.

Never will I barter virtue for unjust gain.

XXII
(111)

Κέχυται πόλις ὑψίπυλος κατὰ γᾶν.

The high-gated city has been laid low upon the ground.

XXIII
(121)

Γαλλαὶ μητρὸς ὀρείης φιλόθυρσοι δρομάδες,
αἷς ἔντεα παταγεῖται καὶ χάλκεα κρόταλα.

The thyrsus-loving, wildly speeding Galli, priests emasculate of the mountain goddess, by whom arms and brazen rattles are clashed.

XXIV

(138)

Οὐ χρυσὸς ἀγλαὸς σπανιώτατος ἐν θνατῶν δυσελ-
 πίστῳ βίῳ, οὐδ' ἀδάμας,
οὐδ' ἀργύρου κλῖναι πρὸς ἄνθρωπον δοκιμαζόμεν'
 ἀστράπτει πρὸς ὄψεις,
οὐδὲ γαίας εὐριπέδου γόνιμοι βρίθοντες αὐτάρκεις
 γύαι,
ὡς ἀγαθῶν ἀνδρῶν ὁμοφράδμων νόησις.

Bright gold is not the thing that is rarest in the sad-hoped life of mortals, nor do steel, nor couches of silver, when tried in comparison with man, nor the heavy-laden fields, fruitful of themselves, of the spacious earth, so shine to the eye as the one-minded spirit of good men.

XXV

(139)

Τύχα, μερόπων
ἀρχά τε καὶ τέρμα· τὺ καὶ σοφίας θακεῖς ἕδρας,
καὶ τιμὰν βροτέοις ἐπέθηκας ἔργοις·
καὶ τὸ καλὸν πλέον ἢ κακὸν ἐκ σέθεν, ἅ τε χάρις
λάμπει περὶ σὰν πτέρυγα χρυσέαν·
καὶ τὸ τεᾷ πλάστιγγι δοθὲν μακαριστότατον τελέθει·
τὺ δ' ἀμαχανίας πόρον εἶδες ἐν ἄλγεσιν,
καὶ λαμπρὸν φάος ἄγαγες ἐν σκότῳ, προφερεστάτα
 θεῶν.

Fortune, that art to mortals both beginning and end, thou dost hold the seats of wisdom, and dost crown the doings of men with glory. And the good from thee is more than the ill, and grace shines about thy golden wing, and that which has been given by thy scales comes to most esteem for happiness. Thou discernest a way out of helpless straits in grief, and bringest a bright light in darkness, O best of deities.

XXVI
(140)

Κλωθὼ Λάχεσίς τ' εὐώλενοι
κοῦραι Νυκτός,
εὐχομένων ἐπακούσατ', οὐράνιαι χθόνιαί τε
δαίμονες ὦ πανδείμαντοι·
πέμπετε δ' ἄμμιν ῥοδόκολπον
Εὐνομίαν λιπαροθρόνους τ' ἀδελφάς, Δίκαν
καὶ στεφανηφόρον Εἰράναν·
πόλιν τε τάνδε βαρυφρόνων
λελάθοιτε συντυχιᾶν.

Clotho and Lachesis, fair-armed daughters of Night, hearken to our prayer, dread goddesses of heaven and the under-world; and send to us rosy-bosomed Order, and her bright-throned sisters, Justice and garland-wearing Peace, and may ye make this city to forget its sorrowful fortunes.

XXVII
(141)

Μισέω μνάμονα συμπόταν.

I hate a boon-companion who remembers.

XXVIII

(143)

Fate

Χὤπερ μόνον ὀφρύσι νεύσῃ,
καρτερὰ τούτῳ κέκλωστ' ἀνάγκα.

And whatsoever it but confirms with its nod, by that mighty necessity is woven.

XXIX

(Bergk, p. 739.)

Ποῦ γὰρ τὰ σεμνὰ (κεῖνα); ποῦ δὲ Λυδίης
μέγας δυνάστης Κροῖσος ἢ Ξέρξης βαρὺν
ζεύξας θαλάσσης αὐχέν' Ἑλλησποντίας;
ἅπαντες ἀΐδαν ἦλθον καὶ λάθας δόμους.

For where are those glories? And where is Croesus, the great lord of Lydia, or Xerxes that yoked the stubborn neck of the Hellespont? All are gone to Hades, and to the abodes of forgetfulness.

www.ingramcontent.com/pod-product-compliance
Lightning Source LLC
Chambersburg PA
CBHW020832230426
43666CB00007B/1199